Finding a Job After Losing Your Way

Stories of Successfully Employed Ex-offenders

Terry Pile

FINDING A JOB AFTER LOSING YOUR WAY:
Stories of Successfully Employed Ex-offenders

Copyright © 2016 by Terry Pile

Cover Design by Molly Gruninger

Published by Career Advisors Resource Center

Contents

INTRODUCTION

G illian C. was a paralegal working for a large technology company, responsible for purchasing millions of dollars worth of domain names on the corporate credit card.

David H. was raised by a single, working mother in a low-income neighborhood in Seattle. By the time he was in middle school, he was an active gang member.

Anna K. immigrated from the Soviet Union as a political refugee. With a master's degree in bilingual education, she was hired for a high-level position in a well-respected, Northwest nonprofit.

What do these individuals with diverse cultural and educational backgrounds have in common? Each has committed a felony and faced formidable challenges re-entering the job market as an ex-offender.

In 2006, I was hired by the King County Jobs Initiative to teach job finding strategies to individuals who have been convicted of crimes and cannot pass the background checks that are prerequisites for most good jobs. Once these students complete my job readiness workshop, they receive additional vocational training and/or assistance in finding jobs from various social service agencies. Many of the students who completed my workshop stay in contact with me, keep me posted of their job search activities and express gratitude when they find employment. Each has touched my heart and allowed me to celebrate their success by sharing their struggles and accomplishments with others.

The 11 individuals profiled in *Finding a Job After Losing the Way* come from diverse socio/economic backgrounds and professions. Their crimes range from drug trafficking, assault with a deadly weapon, child pornography and bank robbery to white collar crimes such as identify theft, extortion and mail fraud. Some have spent years in prison and others were convicted of misdemeanors and committed to home confinement. What they all have in common is a tarnished background that makes finding employment fraught with rejection, humiliation and disappointment.

In November 2010, the Center for Economic and Policy Research released a study titled "Ex-offenders and the Labor Market," which found that a felony conviction or imprisonment significantly reduces the ability of ex-offenders to find jobs, costing the U.S. economy an estimated $57 billion to $65 billion annually in lost economic output.[1] Research also shows that 80 to 90 percent of employers said they would hire former welfare recipients with little recent work experience, but only 40 percent said they would consider hiring job applicants with criminal histories.[2]

Even without criminal backgrounds, many of us have learned over the last few years, that finding employment is hard work. The 2008 recession, ever changing technology, age discrimination and other factors have hampered the most highly qualified and educated job seekers. It is easy to understand why more than 40 percent of ex-convicts commit crimes within three years of their release and wind up back behind bars.[3]

Considering these statistics, I am in awe my former students who did find employment and are successfully rebuilding their lives. How did they motivate themselves each day to get up and look for work? What strategies did they use? How did they answer questions about their misdeeds? How did they learn to cope with rejection after rejection?

Employment for the 11 individuals profiled in this book is an astounding testament to their resilience and perseverance. I am grateful they were willing to confide in me and share their job experiences—both blunders and victories.

Note: Personal details such as names, employers and in some cases, occupations have been changed to protect the privacy of this book's contributors. Their courage and strategies for obtaining employment remain unaltered.

---

1 Prison Legal News, Oct. 18, 2013, *Study Shows Ex-offenders Have Greatly Reduced Employment Rates*
2 Ibid
3 Ibid

About the King County Jobs Initiative

The King County Jobs Initiative (KCJI) is a nationally recognized program that helps ex-offenders prepare for, find and keep living wage jobs. The focus of KCJI is on providing job training in employment areas that have the most potential for wage growth such as truck driving, hazardous waste abatement or other in demand jobs in the trades. It also assists with job placement and supportive services to ensure the client's long-term success. In 2010, the King County Jobs Initiative program received the Washington state governor's Best Practices Award. I share a tiny part of that success. Before individuals can qualify for the program, they must attend my four-day workshop on preparing for employment. If they attend all four days, arrive on time, come prepared and complete the assigned work, they can enter the KCJI job training program. This has been a wonderful opportunity to meet and share the employment successes of many of the individuals you will read about in this book.

How to use this book

The first 11 chapters of this book are profiles of individuals who have struggled to find employment because they were convicted of breaking the law. In some cases the offenses were minor. In others, felonies were committed and the offender spent many years behind bars. In all cases, these individuals have successfully overcome negative background checks, low self-esteem and an unforgiving job market to reenter the world of work and lead productive lives.

In addition to providing inspirational stories, each chapter offers insight from the ex-offender on what he/she did to cope emotionally during a difficult job search. Handling rejection, building a support group and gaining self-esteem are common threads in their narratives.

As a professional career counselor, I have identified the practical themes and strategies that helped these job hunters move forward to successfully gain employment. This advice is summarized at the end of each chapter and will benefit others who find themselves in similar situations. In the final chapter called *Postscripts,* I have included anecdotal stories that took place in class or were related back to me, and offer a valuable tip or insight that will be helpful to readers and reinforce the advice given in previous chapters.

One of the repeated concerns of the individuals profiled in this book was the difficulty in finding resources in a highly fragmented social service system. Their success, in part, was their ability to persevere in finding the services they needed whether it was emotional, legal, financial, educational or employment related. At the end of this book is a list of websites selected to help readers locate national, state and local resources that may be useful in finding a job after losing the way.

Chapter 1
ADAM M.
Allowing help to help.

"All the world is full of suffering. It is also full of overcoming."
—Helen Keller

The National Runaway Safeline estimates that on any given night, there are approximately 1.3 million homeless youth living unsupervised on the streets, in abandoned buildings and with friends or strangers. Adam was one of these youth who considered the parks, viaducts and hidden stairwells around Seattle his home off-and-on for almost sixteen years. Abandoned by his father, Adam and his brother, two and a half years younger, suffered severe neglect and abuse by their profoundly mentally ill mother. By age 12, Adam was chronically running away from home. He and his brother often spent nights in newspaper boxes left in grocery store parking lots, quietly giggling when a load of newspapers was dumped on their heads.

By 7th grade, Adam was removed from his mother's custody and became a ward of the state. Often he was camped out in the DSHS office for as long as three days at a time while staff tried to find him transitional housing, a difficult placement for someone his age. In and out of group and foster homes, Adam felt more comfortable on the streets. If someone took away his shoes for the night to keep him from running away, it didn't matter. Adam ran off in his socks. Although his formal education was nonexistent because of his unstable living situation, he became a savvy student of the street life. He created a street family of youth like himself and was stealing food, clothing and cars. Taking drugs was also a way to numb the hurt and anger Adam felt toward his parents, Child Protective Services, the foster care system and society in general. All had let him down.

Living on the streets was a natural path to prison, and Adam was not a stranger to the criminal justice system. He once remarked on the unusually large size of his case file to a parole officer. "This is only half of it," was the response. In and out of juvenile detention, correctional facilities and prisons, Adam graduated parole for the first time at age 29.

Adam's ascent from the streets began with his involvement in the Washington State Drug Offender Sentencing Alternative system (DOSA). This program allowed judges to sentence certain individuals to reduced prison time in exchange for completing substance abuse treatment. When he reported to the Daily Reporting Center, the officers responsible for monitoring his activities seemed to take an active interest in what he was doing. "Instead of feeling policed, I felt parented," said Adam. It was a feeling he sorely lacked growing up.

Simultaneously, Adam got involvement with a 12-Step Recovery program. His regular participation in 12-step meetings was a way of staying clean. He found it also helped him to stay connected to others with challenging backgrounds. After nine years in recovery, he continues to attend these meetings. He takes great pride in mentoring various members with the hope that they can avoid his mistakes. He is highly sought after as a mentor.

"Attending these meetings taught me a lot—how to show up on time, sit quietly, and most important, how to be of service to others. I was starting to develop some of the habits that came naturally to 'normal people' who led productive lives."

It was a girlfriend who suggested he apply for financial aid to go back to school and a parole officer who encouraged him. Considering it an easy way to support himself, Adam returned to the classroom for the first time since 7th grade with a two-year, full scholarship at a community college. In addition, Adam supported himself by working in food service as a waiter, often taking on two jobs at a time.

Originally motivated by financial aid incentives, Adam found he enjoyed being in school and learning. He discovered he was especially good at writing and public speaking. He also had a strong interest in public policy related to the criminal justice system. A couple of his instructors took a personal interest in him and encouraged his academic pursuits. Rather than feeling marginalized as he had on the streets, he was beginning to feel humanized. After completing general studies requirements at a two-year college, Adam transferred to a distinguished private university. In 2007, he earned a four-year degree in Public Administration & Criminal Justice Policy, graduating cum laude. He laughed, "I was invited to attend school on the same grounds where I had spent many nights as a homeless teenager."

As a student of the streets, Adam had developed keen observational skills and was sensitive to body language, tone of voice and how people carried themselves in different settings. Like a chameleon, he learned how to blend in and adapt to his surroundings. This not only proved useful to his survival in prison, but also to his success in school and work. He observed his instructors, peers, mentors and other professionals to learn how to dress, speak and carry himself. As his confidence grew, so did his willingness to shed his resentment toward "the system." He allowed himself to be open to others who wanted to see him succeed, including case managers, parole officer, attorneys and judges.

A year before graduation, Adam was volunteering as a youth group facilitator at a juvenile correctional facility in the same state system he was once thrust into. He coordinated with corrections officials to provide drug and alcohol recovery workshops to incarcerated youth, a population he has tremendous affinity for. Shortly after graduation, he got involved as a recruiter for adult mentors for youth and children at a local child mentoring organization. He has worked as a housing case manager for ex-offenders and recovery clients and is currently doing similar work for youth at risk. At night, he continues to supplements his income by working as a waiter in an upscale restaurant. He is determined to get his student loans paid off within a year and is considering enrolling in law school.

In addition, to his work with youth, Adam has been invited to sit on several boards working closely with government officials to craft policies in support of homeless and sexually exploited children as well as chemical dependency services. An eloquent speaker, he caught the attention of government administrators and elected officials who arranged for Adam to speak at state and national law enforcement and policy conferences as a key note speaker.

It was Adam's curiosity that led him to follow-up on an email blast announcing the King County Job Readiness program. Without prompting he showed up to my workshop. Immediately, he made an impression on me as someone who was bright and articulate, with a sincere passion for helping marginalized populations. He also inspired the other students in class. So much so, that I hired him to help assist and eventually facilitate future workshops. His energy and job finding acumen are assets to the program.

Adam is still pondering how he wants to architect his future. Although he has had several job offers, he continues to search for the right fit. His goal is to find a way to a way to leverage his numerous community activities, board positions and social service projects into a sustainable career that will allow him work independently and be a positive force in the lives of others who have been neglected and marginalized.

Comments from Adam:

Being acknowledged as a human being who has value and something to contribute was significant in turning my life around. As parole officers, judges and professors took an interest in me, I realized I was no longer invisible.

Learning to shift my perspective and trust others was also a critical component in my transition from the streets to being a productive member of society. I call it, "an attitude of gratitude." By allowing others to help and guide me, I felt empowered and learned how to be self-sufficient, in a positive way. In turn, I am able to help others who are struggling to overcome difficult personal histories.

Advice from Terry:

Create your brand.

When I hear about a new Disney movie, I think of wholesome family entertainment. When I see a Mercedes Benz commercial, wealth and luxury come to mind. And when I think about Adam M., I think of a bright, high energy young man who is passionate about advocating for at-risk youth and other disenfranchised populations. Adam worked hard to change his brand from a chronic ex-offender and drug addict to a respected social service professional committed to being of service to others.

How others perceive you is what people in marketing call your brand. A personal brand is the public image you want to create. It is how we market ourselves to others, particularly employers. Creating your brand should not be an afterthought, a half-baked idea right before a job interview or a string of adjectives to impress an employer. It requires introspection and reflects your values, personal traits, training and marketable skills.

Your personal branding statement (I often refer to it as your commercial) should be one to three sentences that sum up your personal reputation and the value you to bring to an employer.

Here is an example of Adam's branding statement or commercial:

"I am an energetic social services professional dedicated to empowering displaced people to achieve self-sufficiency and independence through gainful employment. I have a bachelor's degree in public administration and criminal justice policy and experience working as a case manager and program administrator. My strengths are my ability to build trusting relationship and offer encouragement and resources to individuals facing multiple barriers to employment."

Are you a fanatic about being on time? Do you go out of your way for others? Is safety in the work place your number one priority? These are values and personal traits that help define who you are and make up your brand. Combine these values and traits with your work experience and training, and you are well on your way to creating your unique brand.

Consider these questions as you begin shaping your branding statement.

1. What are your career goals? How do you want to make a difference?
2. What have you done to support these goals by way of training and experience?
3. How would others positively describe your personal traits and abilities?

Think like an employer.

Adam developed a keen sense of observation having lived on the streets and waited on tables. This ability has benefitted him in his personal and professional life. Through actively listening and observing, he is skilled at anticipating the needs of restaurant patrons. He is also able to pick up subtle cues from employers and respond accordingly. His behavior, body language, appearance and narrative are carefully crafted to fit in with his audiences whether he is in an interview, attending a 12-step meeting, speaking before a conference of policy makers or teaching a job readiness training class.

A common mistake most job hunters make is to think like a job hunter. They are focused on selling themselves but often overlook what the employer is actually buying. For example, if you are applying for a job with a florist, the employer probably doesn't care that you are a certified cosmetologist skilled at cutting hair. But if you can show that your creativity in hair design transfers to unique floral arrangements that will attract new customers, then you have an interested employer.

When an employer is looking at your resume and conversing with you in an interview, he is thinking, "What's in it for me to hire this person? How can she make or save me money, solve my problems and reduce my stress?"

If you are thinking like an employer, you will come prepared with examples to share that show the value you can bring to the job.

Choose your words and information purposefully.

Adam is an inspiring public speaker and has presented nationally to a variety of professional groups. He puts a lot of thought into the words he uses depending on his audience. He knows words like "felon" or "convict" are highly charged words and will use them for shock value if appropriate. If he needs something softer he will refer to "the ex-offender population" or "individuals who have broken the law." These words are not as loaded and are more acceptable to the general public.

People who have a criminal record may have gone to jail, but that in and of itself doesn't tell us who they are. It doesn't define their skills, interest and other contributions. Saying someone is a felon makes it a marker of their identity, whereas saying a person has broken the law humanizes them and implies that they have done other things besides breaking the law.

For example, if I were an employer and you told me you were incarcerated for assault, I would have a lot of reservations about hiring you. I would be thinking you are a violent person, someone with anger management issues. If you said you got in trouble for getting into a fight, that is a scenario I can to relate to. Most people have been at a party or in a bar where a friend drank a little too much and lost control. I would chalk your fight up to a temporary lapse in judgment and consider giving you a chance at a job.

The information you include in your written tools such as job applications, resumes and cover letters, should also be carefully crafted, highlighting your strengths and the value you bring to the employer. No one should be able to tell from reading your resume that you were fired from a job, incurred a workplace injury or did time in prison.

One of the biggest mistakes job candidates make in a job interview is to talk too much. Employers know people are uncomfortable with dead space. If there is a long pause in the conversation, the job candidate will want to fill in, and more often than not, say something he regrets. If you sense you are starting to ramble, just stop and say to the interviewer, "Did

I answer your question? Is there anything else you would like to know?" Turning the conversation back to the interviewer will prevent you from saying more than you intended and move the interview forward.

Some career counselors will tell job candidates to take control of the interview. I think this is bad advice. However, you can—and should—take control of the information you provide to people and the choice of words you use. Adam mastered this after time spent observing and practicing. You can do it, too.

The Take-aways:

✓ Be open to those who want to help

✓ Empower yourself with "an attitude of gratitude," by giving back

✓ Create your brand

✓ Think like an employer

✓ Be mindful of the words and information you use

Chapter 2
PATRICK C.
Make a plan and work it.

"A goal without a plan is just a wish."
—Antoine de Saint-Exupéry

I am always curious about what kinds of books my students are attracted to if they read for pleasure. More often than not, they are reading the Bible or a self-help book. Therefore, I was somewhat surprised when Patrick told me he was reading *The Bartender's Tale*, a work by Ivan Doig, one of my favorite authors. Patrick explained to me that he became a fan of literary fiction while in prison. His mother sent him boxes of books, and later they would discuss them, having formed a two-person book club. But it wasn't just his reading proclivity that drew me to Patrick. He was engaged, articulate and seemed to have his act together, which was an inspiration to everyone taking my job readiness workshop.

Patrick was born in the mid-West in 1970. But a year later, his parents and another family packed up their belongings in a Volkswagen minivan and drove across the country to settle in the Puget Sound area. Patrick's parents were white collar professionals. Every few years, the family upgraded homes, moving to various communities in north Seattle or east of Lake Washington. Patrick was very close to his parents and his younger sister.

By the late 1980s, Patrick had graduated from high school and was enrolled in business and marketing classes at a local community college. He worked in the shipping/receiving department of a home improvement store while attending school. This was during the Clinton era when the economy was enjoying rapid economic growth. The housing industry, in particular, was booming with the rise of subprime and adjustable rate mortgages combined with the lowering of lending standards. This meant just about anyone could secure a loan to buy a house. A friend of Patrick convinced him he could earn a substantial income working in the money lending business. In 1991, Patrick left school and his job and partnered with his friend to start a mortgage refinancing company, Maplewood Mortgages.

From the start, Maplewood Mortgages profited from selling zero-down, no- income verification loans. As Patrick's disposable income grew, he started using recreational drugs. Eventually he was importing and selling drugs from Mexico. While the mortgage loan and the drug import businesses both proved to be lucrative ventures, the work schedules of the two were in direct conflict. Patrick found that selling mortgages during the day and drugs at night was too physically demanding. The decision about where he should put his energy was made for him in 2001, when he was busted for drug trafficking. Although he wasn't incarcerated, he did lose his businesses and his house. At about the same time, he contracted a near fatal intestinal infection and was hospitalized.

After two operations and a year of recovery, Patrick had $150 left in the bank. The mortgage industry was just beginning its decline and his expenses were mounting. Being a shrewd businessman, he was able to invest his meager savings in the drug trade and start to rebuild his empire...until he was arrested for a second time. In 2006, he was sentenced to prison for eight years on charges of drug distribution.

"For the first two years of my incarceration, I just slept. I was physically and emotionally exhausted. I gained a lot of weight as well. But then I started taking stock of myself and my situation. I began working out, reading a lot and looking for other ways to improve intellectually."

In addition to devouring the boxes of books sent by his mom, Patrick took advantage of the prison classes. He particularly enjoyed public speaking, but also learned some Spanish and gained practical, hands-on skills. Working in the prison as a safety orderly, he learned to handle hazardous materials, fill out OSHA reports, work in confined spaces, use lock out/tag out procedures, perform electrical work and other valuable skills required for many jobs in the trades.

Patrick was released the spring of 2014. The first three months, he lived in a half-way house and the remainder of the year with his parents, under home confinement. A large part of Patrick's day was spent at a local WorkSource center, a one-stop employment resource center which can be found in all fifty states. He researched resources for ex-offenders and found out about the King County Jobs Initiative. That was Patrick's path to my job readiness class.

It was Patrick's plan to find a vocational program that would help him obtain the training and certifications to become a commercial truck driver. He believed, correctly, this was an in-demand job that would provide a decent income, a modicum of independence and was a field somewhat forgiving to individuals with his criminal background. In theory, it was an excellent plan. However, like many grant-dependent programs, funding was no longer available for Patrick's targeted vocation. Instead of chasing the money and entering a training program that didn't really interest him, Patrick stayed the course. He was able to borrow money from his family, enroll in a month-long program at a local technical school and secure a CDL-Class A driver's license.

With the certification in hand, Patrick felt prepared to begin his job search. "The job readiness training, gave me a good foundation for writing resumes, cover letters and job finding strategies. I also had a good sense of the types of employers to target. I sent out a few resumes and had an excellent response rate."

After a couple of interviews, he accepted a job as a truck driver for Goodwill Industries. Although the schedule was not ideal with a 3:30 a.m. start time, it paid reasonably well, was conveniently located and offered him the experience he needed to establish a respectable job history.

Committed to the job for at least a year, Patrick is starting to save money and plan his next steps. With a background in shipping/receiving, and his current job as a truck driver, he is exploring a future in logistics or supply chain management within the transportation industry. He would also like to use his public speaking skills he acquired in prison. They will serve him well in sales and customer outreach positions. Knowing Patrick, I am convinced that wherever his future takes him, it will be well researched and methodically planned.

Comments from Patrick:

Make a plan and work it. You need to know where you want to go, then plan on how you will get there. Without a plan, you tend to drift, make bad choices and have a lot of false starts.

Don't be afraid to ask for help. There are numerous federal, state and local resources available to help people with criminal backgrounds. Although the funding fell through for the program in which I was enrolled, I was fortunate to have a supportive family that believed in me and helped me get back on my feet. If you don't have that support, keep searching. You will be amazed at the number of programs that are out there to help you find housing, employment, health care and other basics to help you restart your life. Your local employment center, veterans' administration or non-profit agencies such as Goodwill and Salvation Army are good places to start inquiring about services.

Be patient. It takes a while to integrate back into society, especially if you have been confined for several years. Everything changes so fast. When I got out of prison, it seemed like a whole new world from the one I left eight years ago. It is taking me some time to feel comfortable being back in the real world.

Advice from Terry:
Find your career focus.

One of the first questions I ask my students is, "What kind of job are you looking for?" Most tell me they are looking for any job that pays a living wage. This is like planning a trip without a destination. Where do you start?

How should you pack? What road will you take? Finding a job is no different. If you don't have a clear career goal, you will wander aimlessly through a very long job search.

Patrick approached his job search with a specific career focus. He wanted to be a truck driver. He planned to go to truck driving school and obtain a CDL (certified drivers' license). He had a tangible career goal to work with. Together we created a resume, cover letter, branding statement (commercial) and list of potential employers that supported his end goal. Once he got the required training and certifications, his job search was efficient and effective.

Unlike Patrick, many individuals who are incarcerated or unemployed for long periods of time don't know what they can or want to do. Some want to keep their options open. It is fine to have a couple career goals in mind. But it is most efficient to focus on one at a time. So how do you find a career focus?

If you are not sure how your skills and interests fit into the world of work, visit O*Net Online (www.onetonline.org), a partner of the American Job Center Network. Search for the O*NET Interest Profiler http://www.mynextmove.org/explore/ip. It is an online assessment that will help you clarify your interests and how they relate to common occupations. Once you have settled on a few job titles to explore, O*NET will provide you with comprehensive information on the skills, abilities, technology and education required for the job. It will also tell you how fast the occupation is growing (or shrinking), salary information and related job titles.

Another assessment I recommend is the Minnesota State Colleges and Universities website, Iseek. It offers an assessment based on physiologist John Holland's career codes. It matches your interest to six career clusters. http://www.iseek.org/guide/counselors/counselorclustersholland.html

Another way to identify the skills you enjoy using is through your personal stories. Think about something that you have done in your work, volunteer or prison life that you enjoyed doing and did well. Perhaps you built a dog house for your son's new pet, found a better tool that saved your employer time and money, or taught another inmate how to read. Write your story out using a Background, Action, Result format then identify the skills that were required. Here is an example:

Background: While I was working in shipping/receiving we had a new employee who didn't know how to operate a forklift safely and he ran into a couple of pallets damaging some product.

Action: I didn't want the employee to lose his job, but there really was no training program, and I could see he would get into more accidents. I arranged with my boss to work with the employee after hours so I could train him on how to properly operate the forklift and use safety signals to warn pedestrians.

Results: As a result of my training, the employee kept his job and never had another accident. It also saved the employer money because he didn't have to replace damaged goods or deal with accident claims.

Skills involved: operate a forklift; train others; safety aware; team player; take initiative; communicate effectively with manager and coworker

Once you have written out six to eight stories you will see patterns in your skills list and trends in your stories. If several of your stories involve operating machinery you may want to look into manufacturing careers as a machine operator. If teaching others is a predominant theme, a training job could be in your future.

Use prison jobs to your advantage.

One mistake ex-offenders make is to ignore or minimize the work they performed in prison. For many felons I have worked with, this was the only legitimate job they have ever held. If you worked in a kitchen, performed janitorial services or served on a highway clean-up crew, use it on your resume. Not only are you showing that you have marketable skills, but you will also avoid having a work history gap on your resume.

In Patrick's case, he was a safety orderly. His job involved handling hazardous materials, some of which would be recycled. Much of the work he did as an inmate was at Maxwell Air Force Base. On his resume he indicated that he "worked as a safety orderly handling and recycling hazardous materials at Maxwell Air Force Base." It never occurred to employers that he was a prison inmate performing this work. They assumed he was a air force veteran which helped him get his foot in the door.

If you served time in a state institution, then indicate that your employer was, for example, State of Michigan. If you were incarcerated in a federal prison, you could put the name of the facility such as Sheridan FCI or UNICORE. Most employers won't know that FCI stands for Federal Corrections Institution or that UNICORE is the work program for the Bureau of Prisons. Depending on the job title (librarian, event coordinator, learning center assistant) they might assume you were an employee of the institution, not an inmate. If you worked for a contractor of the correctional facility, use the name of the contracted company as your employer. There are many ways to showcase the job skills you acquired in prison, without divulging your inmate status.

Take a survival or bridge job.

When Patrick was ready to go back to work, he carefully considered his options. He knew truck drivers were in demand and employers in this industry were lenient on backgrounds. He also knew he could get the training fairly quickly. Truck driving was not Patrick's dream job or intended long-term career, but a survival job, a practical solution to getting back into the job market, establishing a fresh employment history and earning an income.

Survival jobs, also called bridge jobs, span the gap between careers. Usually temporary, a survival job is like a place holder if you need time out, go back to school or prepare for a new career. If you decide to take on a survival job, give it some careful thought. Survival jobs have many advantages and could be a strategic next step to building a new career.

In Patrick's case, truck driving provides a steady income in addition to developing new skills. It has restored his self-respect and confidence in his ability to be a contributing member of the workforce. Driving a truck is not something Patrick sees himself doing the rest of his working life, but he does see it as a bridge to a job in transportation management, logistics or supply chain management. These are careers that interest Patrick and he wants to consider for his future. His previous warehouse experience and current job as a truck driver serve as a good foundation.

The disadvantage to taking on a survival job while preparing for a new career is that it limits the time you can devote to making a career transition if you put all your energy into making a living wage. If Patrick had taken a survival job as a front desk clerk in a hotel, for example, he would be working full-time at a job that had no relation to his career goals. It would also be more difficult for him to find the time to go back to school and acquire the skills and knowledge for a job in transportation management.

If you are looking for a survival job during a career transition, consider the following:

- Look for survival jobs where you can learn a new skill or enhance a skill that you will need in a future career. If you take a clerical job, look for opportunities to learn new software and databases. Working in a fast food restaurant can lead to supervisory experience in the form of training new employees or standing in for your boss when he/she is off site.
- Apply for survival jobs that relate to an interest or hobby. If you love coffee, going to work as a barista may actually be fun for a change of pace. If you have an interest in fashion, working retail may give you an opportunity to share your flare for style with less talented clients.
- Avoid survival jobs that will zap your energy. Look for

jobs that have weekend and evening shifts and don't require that you bring work home, physically or emotionally. This will free you up to spend the more productive weekday hours pursuing activities to prepare you for your new career like returning to school, participating in an internship or building business connections through volunteering.

- Make sure your resume it a good fit for the survival jobs you are applying for. If the job requires you to operate an NC machine and you don't have the experience, don't waste your time applying with the false hope than an employer will train you.
- Keep up your spirits. Look for anything positive you can take away from the job. Are you saving gas on a short commute? Making new friends? Giving your day some needed structure? Remind your self that the survival job is temporary.

The Take-aways:
- ✓ Be patient. Take time to adjust to your new normal.
- ✓ Don't be afraid to ask your family for help.
- ✓ Get focused on a career goal.
- ✓ Include prison jobs on your resume.
- ✓ Consider a survival or bridge job to get you back in the job market.

Chapter 3
LATRICE G.
Change is possible, if you want it.

"Right now I am trying to be in a place of calm, a place where I can chill out and then handle the chaos of life better. You don't just get it overnight; you have to work at it. It's a daily struggle."
—Jackee Harry

There is something impish about Latrice when you first meet her. Perhaps it is an innocence in her smile contrasted with a spark of mischievousness. She is the type of student who brings treats for her classmates and jokes a lot, so you are not always sure if she is being funny or dead serious. Her fun-loving nature and self-confidence make her highly approachable and caring. The one thing you would never suspect about Latrice is that she has a long history as the perpetrator of domestic violence and assault, claiming unabashedly to have "probably been in 100 fights."

Latrice, part African American, part Cherokee, was born in a Seattle suburb in the early 1980s. She grew up with an older sister, younger brother and working mom. Her dad was an alcoholic who spent a lot of time in prison and was rarely around. Latrice believes it was the lack of a father figure that created the anger inside her. From seventh grade on, she was expelled from every school she attended, usually for bullying or fighting. In her senior year, she dropped out of the alternative school she had been attending and hung around with her brother and his street gang. Needless to say, by then her relationship with her mom and sister had deteriorated.

In her early 20s, Latrice completed her GED, but she found it impossible to hold a steady job and had developed a fatalistic attitude. She was drinking heavily and often depressed, which triggered her angry episodes. Gall bladder surgery and prescription drugs only increased her depression.

There were two defining moments in Latrice's life that saved her, literally and figuratively. The first was a diagnosis of high blood pressure caused by alcohol. Latrice was told by her doctor that if she didn't stop drinking, she would likely die from a stroke at a young age.

The second event was when she was arrested for residential burglary and domestic violence after a fight with a boyfriend. Prior to 2009, her confrontations had been classified as misdemeanors, but this time she spent eight days in jail before being able to post bail and realized she was looking at some real prison time.

"The idea of having a felony on my record was my wake up call," said Latrice. "I also felt as I approached my 30s, that I was getting too old for this kind of behavior. I had a young niece I cared about. I wanted to be her role model, not, Aunt Latrice, the example of what not to do. It was time for some maturing and to make something productive with my life."

Eventually, the charges were dropped to Assault 1, and Latrice was assigned to 150 hours of community service. She stopped drinking, cold turkey, and got into an anger management program. She realized she had the sole responsibility for taking care of herself and she wanted to do it right, regardless of what perceptions others had of her. At the age of 30, she started to think seriously about her life and a sustainable career.

"I always wanted to work in the medical field. But I realized that was not going to happen with my background." Latrice knew that what she needed to do was to stay away from the bad influences in her life and break old habits that got her into trouble. She made amends with her mother and sister, hoping to earn their support and approval. She also began looking at employment programs and connecting with people who were doing the kind of work that she might like, and still earn a living wage.

One day while surfing through Facebook, she saw a posting from her sister's friend, Arthur. He had just completed the King County Jobs Initiative program and was working a job in hazardous material (hazmat) removal. Latrice contacted him to find out more about working in the hazmat field. From what he told her, it sounded like it might be a good fit. She enjoyed working out doors. She didn't mind hard, physical work. She liked the fact that each day was a little different from the day before. But most of all she liked the paycheck. If she could get into the union, she could easily make more than $30 an hour.

Through networking, Latrice eventually found her way to the King County Jobs Initiative and my job readiness class. She was enthusiastic, engaged and generous with her sense of humor. On the last day of class, as was my practice, I offered resume assistance to any former student who might want extra help. I made this offer with the knowledge that although the gesture might be appreciated at the time, it is rarely used.

"You'll be hearing from me, Miss P," Latrice piped up. "I've heard that before," I thought.

About three months later, an email from Latrice showed up in my inbox. She had just completed the hazmat program and, true to her word, was collecting on my promise to help her with her resume. She had made some connections from class and was ready to get the word out that she was looking for hazmat work.

When I last talked to Latrice, she had been employed as an apprentice by a hazmat abatement company for the last six months and held a union card. She was making $32 an hour. (During the slow times she took on warehouse work through a staffing agency.) She talked of climbing 60-foot scaffolds, replacing an old roof at a university, performing containment work at the airport and removing asbestos in some of the buildings at an aerospace company. She loved her work, and hadn't lost her temper once. She had her sights set on earning a few more certifications to have more options and greater marketability. Eventually she wants to get her supervisor's card. Since this requires 6,000 working hours, it is a major commitment for Latrice in developing her career. But knowing Latrice, I can easily see her baking a batch of cookies for the crew of hazmat technicians she is supervising in celebration of their good work.

Comments from Latrice:

You need to find your inner strength. Although I wanted my family to be proud of me, I realized it was most important to first be proud of myself. Family members and friends will soon follow when they see what you have accomplished through shear willpower and hard work.

Another important factor for me is to stay busy. I get to work early and am always looking for things to do when work slows down. Because abatement work is not always steady, I am connected to a staffing agency and can fill in the slow times with warehouse work. It doesn't pay as much, but when you keep busy, you have less opportunity to get into trouble. It's important to have that steady flow of income, not only to pay the bills but to boost your confidence and self-respect.

Advice from Terry:

Look for ex-offender friendly industries and employers.

I was impressed by Latrice's practical approach to her career. She could have tried to get a job in healthcare, her preferred profession, but the effort would have probably ended with rejection and discouragement, in addition to a lot of wasted. She assumed, rightly so, any industry where you are working with vulnerable populations generally will not hire individuals with a criminal record. These industries tend to be healthcare, education, finance, banking, insurance and law. Of course there are always exceptions. Manufacturing, construction, food service, information technology, retail, sports, entertainment and travel/leisure are industries that more forgiving when it comes to hiring individuals with a record. Again there are exceptions from employer to employer, and larger companies usually have more stringent policies.

Increasingly, women are choosing jobs in the trades, although the current rate is about three percent. Jobs in the construction trades provide stable careers, good pay and benefits. In this case a trade job met most of Latrice's criteria. She wanted a profession that was open to someone with her background but also offered versatility and growth potential. Hazardous material removal is not only a growing career, but a well paying one. It can lead to less physically demanding roles such as environmental lab technician, building inspector, site supervisor, safety trainer, and other related careers.

Consider apprenticeship and internship opportunities.

Apprenticeships and internships both give you hands on work experience. Apprenticeships are usually associated with jobs in technology, engineering, construction and the trades. They are longer than internships (some lasting several years) and you get paid while learning and eligibility into a trade union. The work you do is related directly to your occupation.

Internships are often, although not exclusively, tied to college credits. They usually last for a semester and are often in white collar jobs such as marketing, business administration or finance, for example. You generally work for free or a small stipend. The work you do may be more generalize and could range from fetching coffee to managing high level assignments. It is important to do your research prior to accepting an internship so you know what to expect. Internships are often posted online at school career centers.

The advantage of having an internship or apprenticeship is that it gives you real-life work experience. It not only looks impressive on a resume, but also gives you a good feel for your new career. It is a way to make valuable connections and accumulate references when you start looking for your permanent job.

Being a woman has its advantages. The trades are encouraging women to consider non-traditional roles and many offer apprenticeship programs. Check your local union for apprenticeship programs and union eligibility or the organization ANEW—Apprenticeship and Non-Traditional Employment for Women.

Talk to people about their careers.

Once you have explored careers on the Internet, it is wise to talk to people who are actually doing the kind of work that interests you. Latrice found an acquaintance on her Facebook page that went through the King County Jobs Initiative training and was working as a hazmat technician. She made an appointment to discuss his daily responsibilities. By talking to someone in her field of interest, she could ask questions and get a real-life perspective on the pros and cons of the job. Having done her research, she felt she had enough information to make an informed decision about career path.

Social media (LinkedIn, in particular, a professional networking site) is a good way to connect with people and learn about what they do for work. If you found someone performing the kind of work you might want to pursue, don't hesitate to request an information meeting. Face-to-face meetings are the best, but not always possible. Requesting a meeting by phone or online (perhaps through Skype or InstantMessaging) are alternatives.

An information meeting should not be a ruse for an interview. It is a vehicle for gathering information on industries, occupations and employers. Although most workers are extremely busy, many will be willing to take time out to talk to you about what they do if you approach them respectfully and have honest motives.

Request your meeting for a specific length of time (generally 30 minutes) and stick to it. Have thoughtful questions prepared as you are the one in charge of the interview. Toward the end of the meeting, ask if there is anyone else you should talk to. Get permission to use the name of the person you are interviewing to make networking connections. Finally, don't forget to send a thank you note for the interviewee's time and offer to help them if they are ever in need of assistance.

Here are some questions you might consider when conducting an information meeting:

- How did you get into this field?
- What education and qualifications should a person have for the job you are in?
- How do you feel the industry is doing overall? Is it growing or shrinking?
- What is the earning potential for someone in your field?
- Describe a typical day on the job?
- What do you like most or least about your work?
- What kind of advice would you give someone like me who is considering a career in this field?
- Who else do you think I should talk to? May I use your name?

The Take-aways:

✓ Make yourself proud first. When others see your confidence and accomplishments their admiration will follow.

✓ Take time out to identify your strengths and interest to determine how they fit best in the current job market.

✓ Be practical about your career expectations. Know the types of jobs and employers that will be forgiving to someone with a record.

✓ Consider apprenticeships and internships to build your skills and experience.

✓ Set up information meetings with others in occupations that interest you.

Chapter 4
DAVID H.
Don't let your mistakes define you.

"Success is to be measured not so much by the position that one has reached in life, as by the obstacles one has overcome trying to succeed."

—Booker T. Washington

In 2010, the incarceration rate nationwide for white males was 678 inmates for a population of 100,000 residents. For black males, it was six times higher or 4,347[4]. So it isn't surprising that David was arrested within days of his 18th birthday. If you are a black male living in poverty, there is a one in three chance you will have a criminal record by the age of 18[5] and a 40 percent chance you will re-offend.[6] What is more surprising is that David has been able to break out of the cycle and become a well-respected and accomplished member of his community.

David grew up in the 1970s in a low-income neighborhood of Seattle. His mother did not work and his father was not present. By the time he was in middle school he was actively involved in gang activity, hanging around like-minded friends who were lured by material possessions but had no means to acquire them. In 8th grade, he was sentenced to two-years probation for stealing a leather coat from a classmate. By 10th grade, he had dropped out of school and was earning his living on the streets selling drugs. Shortly after turning 18, David was arrested for drug trafficking and sent to a medium security prison for 21 months.

In prison, David completed his GED and found his spiritual self. He became a licensed minister shortly after his release. He also trained as a machinist through a local technical school. But when the economy tanked af-

4 Bureau of Justice Statistics, Pew Research Study, 2010
5 Criminal & Delinquency Study, Jan. 2014
6 Criminal Recidivism: The Plight of American Male Youth, 11/2013; www.psycosocialissues.com

ter 9/11, David lost his job, and faith could not put food on the table or pay the bills. David went back to his former, more lucrative work selling drugs. By 2007, he had been locked up two more times.

I met David in 2009. The economy was still limping along, and he had found his way to the King County Jobs Initiative. After taking my workshop, he entered the Brownfields program, partially funded by the Environmental Protection Agency. The program was designed to train low-income individuals in hazardous material (hazmat) abatement. The work paid well and could lead to union work and union wages. David was enthusiastic about this new career. He had kids to support from a previous marriage and a new girlfriend. The prospect of a well-paying, legitimate career buoyed his spirits.

When David graduated from the five-week Brownfields program, he had earned at least 10 hazmat related certifications and was filled with optimism for his future. However, the construction industry was still sluggish. Hazmat jobs were temporary at best and going to union workers first. David didn't have enough work hours to be eligible to join the union, and without a union card, it was unlikely he would get the experience—the perfect Catch-22 for many people wanting to break into a new career.

It would have been easy to fall back into old habits and return to his former life on the streets to make some quick money, but David's spirit was broken. Instead of selling drugs, he started using and became addicted to powdered cocaine. His girlfriend left him, and the mother of his kids moved in with her parents, making it difficult for David to see his children. He was depressed and physically exhausted.

It was at this point that David had another spiritual awakening. He realized that his life had become a bad cliché, not an example that made him proud or one he wanted his children to emulate. He needed to step outside of this self-made prison. Willing to do whatever it took to turn his life around in a positive way, this time David sought out and received support from his mother. He went into a recovery program to get clean, and lived in a transitional house to put his life back together. At age 37, he was determined to start over.

Through Narcotics Anonymous, David acquired a mentor who directed him to the Community Pathways Program at Goodwill. He immediately enrolled in a six-week program called College 101. The program assisted students in exploring career options, enrolling in vocational or college programs, filing for financial aid and developing good study habits. Through this program, David realized he enjoyed working with youth and had a talent for counseling. As a result, he enrolled at Seattle Central Community College where, in 2013, he earned an Applied Associate of Arts degree in social and human services, and chemical dependency.

He also earned bragging rights for making the Dean's List two consecutive quarters and receiving a Fabien Foundation Scholarship. The scholarship was designed specifically to help individuals who have been incarcerated for more than a year with the financial aid to pursue a field of study. David is now slowly working toward a bachelor's degree in chemical dependency counseling.

In addition to pursuing a college education, at the suggestion of another mentor, David applied for and was hired as a peer specialist at Sound Mental Health. In his 20-hour a week job, he assisted three case managers in working with more than 70 individuals recovering from substance abuse. As a peer specialist, under professional guidance, he met one-on-one with clients and facilitated small groups. He also spoke at public forums and provided referral services as appropriate.

If going to college and working part-time weren't enough to keep him busy, David became active in the No New Jim Crow Seattle Coalition. This campaign is dedicated to ending mass incarceration in America, beginning in Seattle/King County. Through his community activities, such as public speaking, policy writing and relationship building with faith-based groups, David hopes to advance this organization's mission "to encourage creative and nonviolent means to build a society based not on punitive laws, imprisonment, illness and oppression, but on a transformative, compassionate sense of justice and respect for the dignity and well-being of all people." Instead of hanging out on the streets, David now finds himself rubbing shoulders, in a good way, with judges, lawyers, business executives, directors of non-profit programs and religious leaders.

Currently, David has put his education and social service work on-hold. To support his family and make ends meet, he is working for a friend, using his trade skills to restore and refurbish yachts. However, he remains active as a community advocate and organizer, writer, public speaker and gang interventionist. He hopes to influence the many issues related to race-based disparities within the criminal justice system. David is building a strong resume and influential connections that will not only benefit him directly, but also help him to leave a legacy of social justice for his children and his community.

Comments from David:

If you are determined to turn your life around, you need to begin by stepping out of your habits. Next, set realistic goals and don't be in a hurry. Change doesn't happen overnight. Even if you slip, pick yourself up and start over. Give yourself as long as five years. Don't be afraid to share your story and reach out to mentors to hold yourself accountable. Hang where they hang and model their behavior. You can learn from past mistakes and create a new, brighter future for yourself.

Advice from Terry:
Make a commitment to change.

One of the most important lessons to be learned from David's experience is that you can't let your past define you. There are many outside forces that can beat a person down including peer pressure, poverty, absence of role models and a lack of jobs. With these obstacles facing young men and women today, it is no wonder selling drugs or robbing a stranger may seem like an easier, faster way to get your needs and wants met.

Once David wanted to make a change, he knew he needed to step outside his environment. He reconnected with family, got into a rehab program and started seeking out mentors and community services. With the support of his mentors, he was able to identify employment opportunities and resources such as the Goodwill Community Pathways program. This led to continuing his education in a focused way. Obtaining a scholarship and finding related jobs allowed David to channel his energy for the good and helped him to avoid "back sliding" into old habits.

Even though David is not working in his chosen field, he is still working hard. Through his community activism he is always meeting influential people. Often times it is not necessarily what you know but who you know that will bring you to that ultimate job you've been hoping for. David's continuing efforts and his personal connections will, in all probability, be able to further his political agenda as well as his future career goals.

Find a mentor to guide you.

A mentor is an experienced person who will go out of his or her way to help others reach their life goals. An informal mentor will listen, offer advice and provide coaching in a casual, unstructured way. You may have an informal relationship with your mentor indefinitely. A formal mentor agrees to an ongoing, planned partnership with scheduled meetings and a set agenda to help the mentee reach specific goals. Formal mentor/mentee relationships generally last six months to a year.

If you are looking for a mentoring experience, formal or informal, you may be able to find a mentor through the National Mentoring Partnerships program at www.mentoring.org. Many institutions of higher learning, chambers of commerce, religious institutions, 12-Step programs and community centers have mentoring programs as well.

Take advantage of community resources.

David left no stone unturned to a new opportunity. He was very skilled at finding community resources and using them to his advantage. Whether it was financial aid, a vocational program or life-skills training, he benefited from each program in some way. Although using his hazmat skills and working union jobs did not pan out in 2009, he is using many of the skills he acquired from the King County Jobs Initiative in his current work of restoring yachts. The counseling skills he gained through his education and training in social services and peer mentoring are enhancing his volunteer and advocacy work.

If you are looking for community programs and resources to advance your goals, I recommend you begin with these two agencies, United Way and your state's one-stop employment center. United Way will refer you to agencies that can help you further your goals. The employment center staff will know about training programs, financial aid and other resources for which you may be eligible. You can find more information about these agencies in the resource section of this book.

The Take-aways:

- ✓ Your past is not your present. You can change old habits.
- ✓ Step outside your environment. Get involved in community activities.
- ✓ Surround yourself with positive support. Find a mentor.
- ✓ Take advantage of community resources to advance your education and training.
- ✓ If you slip back into old habits, don't beat yourself up. Pick yourself up and start over.

Chapter 5
MARCUS C.
Learning to forgive yourself.

"Mistakes are always forgivable if one has the courage to admit them."
—Bruce Lee

Early one November morning in 2013, Marcus answered a knock at the door. Two police detectives asked if they could come in and ask a few questions. Puzzled, but cooperative, Marcus consented. Two hours later he was handcuffed and taken to police headquarters for the possession and distribution of child pornography.

Marcus was born in Puerto Rico in 1981 to a middle class family. His father was a police officer, and his mother stayed home to raise the children. When Marcus was 16, his parents divorced and his mother moved Marcus and his two siblings to Arizona, where they lived with relatives until she found employment.

Marcus was a good student and ambitious. He earned a four-year degree in accounting from the University of Arizona and studied at the American University in Paris. After graduating in 2009, he moved to Seattle at the advice of a friend and shortly after his arrival, he was hired for a position in the accounting department of a software development company.

The move to Seattle agreed with Marcus. He had a well-paying job, a nice place to live and made lots of friends. He also found Seattle's liberal politics compatible with his gay lifestyle. For the next three years, Marcus worked hard and partied hard. It was a good life for a young man in his early 30s with few responsibilities.

But these pluses turned into a big minus at some point between May and September of 2013. Because Marcus hosted frequent parties, it wasn't uncommon to find friends and strangers wandering through his house on weekends of drinking and camaraderie. Generous and trusting, Marcus never thought too much of it. However, at some point, one of his guests helped himself to Marcus's computer and created a sky drive account using an IP address linked to Marcus's location. Soon he was uploading and distributing files with pornographic content. Although Marcus eventually discovered the files, he never gave them much thought—until the police found them in his possession.

Eventually, the perpetrator was identified, but just the fact that Marcus was in possession of such content was incriminating, and he pleaded guilty. After six days in jail, Marcus was able to round up the bail money from his friends—just in time to avoid relocation to the "Gladiator Zone" of the King County jail, a place associated with gangs and violence.

For the next six months, Marcus remained under house arrest with the condition he see a treatment provider. He was also eligible for work release and found an accounting job working for a local health food distributor. He was in the job almost eight months, when the owner learned of his background and asked him to leave. Shortly after his dismissal, Marcus was diagnosed as HIV positive.

Unemployed, with a criminal record, struggling with his sexuality and health issues, Marcus felt his life had collapsed, and he experienced tremendous shame. He referred to this period as "the Dark Days." Understandably, he fell into depression and struggled to move forward. Unfortunately, the first therapist Marcus was assigned to did little to bolster his confidence and was more harmful than helpful. With the support of his attorney, Marcus insisted on making a change and found a therapist with whom he was more compatible. "This therapist was better able to understand the issues I was dealing with. He served as an advocate rather than an adversary. That first counselor made me feel terrible, and I didn't need that. I was hard enough on myself."

In addition to therapy, Marcus was committed to avoiding alcohol and drugs. His focus was on his health. He started attending Alcoholics

Anonymous and Narcotics Anonymous meetings. "It helped me to hear other people's stories and how they were coping. I found it very motivational and made some close friends."

Finding the King County Jobs Initiative also played an important role in turning Marcus's life around. On the first day of class, he was still depressed and lacked confidence. However, it was clear to me that this polite, quiet, young man had the professionalism, intelligence and list of accomplishments that were sure to impress most employers. During the next four days, Marcus was extremely attentive, asked lots of questions and took notes profusely. After class, he followed up with emails once or twice to ask job-search questions.

About a year later, when I contacted Marcus to be interviewed for this book, he was three months into his new job, with full benefits, as an accountant for a small food products manufacturer. He loved his new job, was in good health and living alone in a comfortable apartment. He also had a new partner whom he had met at a support group. This relationship made him very happy, but he was taking things slowly. He was still healing emotionally and learning to forgive himself.

As I probed Marcus about his job search, I was stunned by his response. He had followed my job-finding advice word for word. He told me that after my class he had printed up business cards which he used for networking. Next, he created a resume and cover letter template he customized for each job he applied for. Then he made a marketing plan, a target list of employers in industries that he thought would be "ex-offender friendly." Those were the websites he studied and monitored for job openings.

He also prepared his "commercial," or the script he would use when responding to questions about his background. This had caused him problems in past job interviews. Now he was prepared to respond to the difficult questions about his record without stumbling or being embarrassed.

Marcus had even made up a skills portfolio, a binder that contained examples of his work. He shared this with employers during the interviews.

He included his resume, professional credentials and several Excel reports and graphs he had created in other jobs. Job candidates in creative professions often bring work portfolios to job interviews, but for an accountant, this was most unusual and very impressive.

Marcus had applied for numerous jobs without results, prior to taking my job readiness training workshop. After taking the class, he spent a few weeks researching companies, customizing his materials and applying for jobs. Within a few weeks he had two phone interview, two in-person interviews and a job offer.

"I love my job and the people I work with. My boss is amazing. She knows about my past, but it doesn't seem to matter. She is all about moving forward and that is exactly what I am doing."

Comments from Marcus:

Forgive yourself and allow yourself a second chance. This was hard for me, and I am still working on it. But each day it gets a little better. Also, be willing to share with others and show you are making a difference. Consider volunteering or finding a group where your presence can be a positive force.

Advice from Terry:
Take care of yourself mentally and physically.

Marcus had serious emotional and physical hurdles to overcome, but he made it a priority to deal with these issues before attempting to look for a job.

If you are not emotionally and physically ready to return to work, employers will quickly sense it. Depression is one of the most common barriers to employment facing job hunters of all backgrounds.

"Some 20 percent of the long-term unemployed say they are depressed or being treated for depression—twice as many as those unemployed for five weeks or less, according to a Gallup-Healthways Well-Being Index survey released in June (2014)." 7 Here are some tips for keeping in

---

7 "The Unemployed Psyche," Jennifer Libreto, CNN Money, Aug. 8, 2014

shape mentally and physically.

Seek mental health counseling and/or join a support group. Reaching out to others will help you feel less isolated and reinforce that your situation is not unique.

Develop a daily routine and stick to it. Providing structure to your day will prevent you from oversleeping. Get up and get dressed at the same time each day. Set aside a specific time for your job search, running errands and doing a hobby or activity that you enjoy.

Exercise. This will keep you physically healthy and mentally acute. Build exercise into your daily regime whether it is going to a fitness club, riding a bike or taking a walk around the block.

Eat healthy foods and get a good night's sleep. Don't use junk food as comfort food. Avoid napping during the day and go to bed each night at the same time.

Don't take rejection personally. Each "no" gets you closer to a "yes."

Taking good care of your mental and physical health will improve the way you feel about yourself. You will radiate confidence, and perform better in interviews. Employers will notice.

Surround yourself with positive people.

Creating your own cheering gallery is easier said than done after you have been convicted of a crime. Although one would hope family and friends will be there for you, that isn't always the case. Whether it is lack of trust, embarrassment or guilt, family and friends can't be counted on to provide the positive support you need at this time, and can often bring you down.

Marcus had very specific issues to deal with related to his health and sexuality. His family members, although supportive, either lived far away or had their own families to take care of. He didn't want to be a burden to them. He also wanted to avoid old friends, as they represented a past he wanted to forget. He was determined to start over.

As a condition of his treatment, Marcus was assigned to therapy. One would expect a mental health professional to be the lynchpin of your support group, but in this case, the therapist had a negative impact on Marcus's self-esteem. Fortunately, he had the wherewithal to advocate for himself. He found a therapist who was a better fit and a 12-Step group who offered unconditional support.

If you lack positive support from family and friends, you needn't feel alone. There are many resources and support groups to help ex-offenders reintegrate into the community. Some are faith-based, others are government programs or sponsored by non-profit groups. A list of resources can be found at the back of this book. I encourage you to explore it.

Mary Renault, the English novelist said, "How can people trust the harvest, unless they see it sown?" Earning back trust in those you care about is not always easy, but it can be done if your actions demonstrate you are sincere and committed to moving forward in a positive way.

Rise above your competition.

Marcus had been struggling with his job search with less than satisfactory results. He was proactive about looking for help and through his research learned about the King County Jobs Initiative. He understood the value of seeking professional advice and was methodical about applying what he learned.

After taking the job readiness workshop, Marcus took an inventory of his job search and marketing tools, evaluating them from a new perspective. He knew they were dull and needed sharpening.

First he researched companies and industries that were more likely to hire ex-offenders. Originally he had been targeting accounting firms without success. He started looking at companies in the manufacturing industry. They needed accountants, too, he realized. A whole new set of possibilities opened up for him.

Next he punched up his resume which he felt was too general and didn't adequately show his value. He highlighted his accomplishments in greater detail and quantified the results. For example, instead of the statement, "made recommendations to reduce costs," he quantified the results by stating, "reduced cost of shipping by 15 percent by recommending a new transportation vendor." He also customized his cover letters to make them less generic and more personal for each employer. In the opening paragraph of the cover letter, he explained why he wanted to work for the company and what made him a good fit.

Here are some other actions Marcus took to set himself apart from the competition. I call them the icing on the cake. They are necessary for a successful job search, but they are somewhat out of the ordinary and helped separate Marcus from other job candidates in a good way.

Business Cards:

Business cards date as far back as the 15th century and were used to announce a social visit. They were referred to as visiting or calling cards. Although the calling card has vanished, business cards are still one of the most popular advertising tools for personal and professional use. What should you put on your card? Most people put their name, contact information and professional career goal. Some will even include their branding statement or commercial on the front or back of the card. You want your card to have a clear message and an easy way for people to contact you. If you are savvy on a computer, you can buy business card stock for about $10 and print our own cards. There are many online services, like Vista Print, www.visitprint.com, where you can have cards made that are professional looking and inexpensive. Remember to keep your business cards with you at all times. You never know when a networking opportunity will show up.

Skills Portfolio:

A skills portfolio is a visual representation of your skills, knowledge and experience. It is a marketing tool that will give your current or future employers a positive perspective on your contribution to their future. It is usually a three-ring binder that includes samples of the variety and quality of your work. It is typical for artists, photographers and event planners to have a skills portfolio because their work is so visual. If you are a receptionist or electrician, you may be wondering what you would put in your skills portfolio. As an accountant, Marcus added spreadsheets he created, reports he wrote and photos of the companies he worked for to provide visual interest. Below are additional suggestions:

- Credentials. Start with your resume. Add any certifications, licenses, school transcripts or list of classes you completed that are required for your profession.
- Work samples. Include reports you have written, spreadsheets you prepared, fliers or safety posters you created. Consider including logos of former employers you worked for or any photos you might have or can recreate of you doing your job.
- Testimonials. These are the awards, 'atta boys', performance evaluations and letters of recommendation.

Now you know what to do with those certificates you earned after completing your First Aid/CPR class or got your CDL. Keep them in an archive until you are ready to build your skills portfolio for the next interview.

Thank you notes:
The first thing Marcus did after each interview was send a thank you note. He expressed his interest in working for the company, reminded the interviewer why he would be a good fit and sincerely thanked the employer for her consideration.

Not long ago I was presenting a workshop on "interviewing skills" to a very diverse group of individuals who were looking for work. When I broached the subject of sending a thank you note after an interview, one former assembly line worker said incredulously, "Why would somebody like me write a thank you note? Nobody does that in my line of work." A woman who had experience hiring assembly line workers interjected, "That is exactly why you should do it. If nobody else does, you would certainly stand out in my mind."

What ever happened to old fashion courtesy? It use to be common practice for people to send thank you notes after an interview, but it is much less in vogue today. Sending a thank you note for a receiving a referral, job lead, information meeting or interview is a must. It is an additional opportunity to sell your benefits, address specific concerns that may have come up in a meeting, demonstrate your interest in the company and display your professionalism. Plus, it is the polite thing to do if someone does something nice on your behalf.

The thank you note can take a variety of forms. It can be an email, letter or hand written card depending on the culture of the organization or industry. The most important thing to remember about a thank you note is that to be effective it must have substance. The thank you note should include a statement about why you want to work for the company, a reminder of the benefits you have to offer (your commercial) and a sincere thank you for the interviewer's time and consideration.

Getting a job today is all about standing out. Writing an influential thank you note is another opportunity to separate yourself from the crowd. Besides, it would make your mother proud.

The Take-aways:
- ✓ Learn to forgive yourself.
- ✓ Take care of yourself emotionally and physically.
- ✓ Reach out to others and give back in return.
- ✓ Seek professional advice regarding your job search.
- ✓ Reevaluate and sharpen your job search tool kit.
- ✓ Write a thank you note after an interview.

Chapter 6
GILLIAN C.
Perseverance has its pay off.

"It doesn't matter how slowly you go, as long as you do not stop."
—Confucius

When I first met Gillian in my job readiness class, I liked her immediately. She was cheerful, engaged and not afraid to challenge my advice, in a respectful way. She was also good at finding typos in my workbook. I wondered, what was this bright, young women doing in a class for ex-offenders?

After four intense six-hour days in a classroom, you learn a lot about your students, and Gillian's back-story finally came to the forefront. She was a graduate of a Washington state university with a degree in political science. Shortly out of college, she went to work in the customer service department for an international technology company. She gradually got promoted to account representative and at one point, the company paid for her to become a certified paralegal to better enable her to assist the corporate legal department.

Gillian continued to move into positions with added responsibility and was eventually promoted to program manager for the company's domain program. Each time the company came out with a new software product for a client, she handled the purchase of domain names. As a way of concealing the company name from domain-name sellers, she was encouraged to use her own corporate credit card. At one point, she was responsible for 22,000 domain names worth more than $15 million dollars.

As Gillian's career ascended, there were increasing pressures at work and home. In addition to putting in longer hours, her older brother, with whom she was very close, died of a heart attack. Other family members were having money problems and leaning on Gillian for financial support. Although she was making a decent income, family issues continued to weigh on her. Without giving it too much thought, she began using her corporate credit card to make personal purchases with the notion of reimbursing the company when she handed in her expense reports.

Gillian's good intensions to repay her employer fell by the wayside when she realized that the company's internal controls were not sophisticated enough to separate personal from corporate expenses. Her slightly padded expense report cleared the system undetected. It was almost like binging on your favorite ice cream. You tell yourself, I'll do it just once and make up for the extra calories tomorrow. Only the next day you tell yourself, a little more can't hurt. Yet the calories start adding up.

Eventually a client began questioning itemized costs on invoices. A financial investigation ensued, and Gillian's employer started asking tough questions. In 2005, Gillian was called into the Human Resources Director's office and fired for inflating her expense reports. The company took it one step farther and decided to prosecute, using Gillian as a cautionary tale to others in the company who might be tempted to engage in similar practices.

In 2008, Gillian was charged with extortion and mail fraud and released on her own recognizance. Because of her paralegal background, she was able to help her attorney prepare for her defense and keep legal fees down. As she began adding up unauthorized expenses, she was shocked to find that over a four-year period, she had spent close to a million dollars of her employer's money.

"There was nothing to show for it," she said. "I didn't buy luxury items or take fancy trips. I did give some of the money to family, and I must have used the rest to pay bills. The money just disappeared. I can't imagine what I was thinking at the time."

To this day, Gillian is still not sure how she could have considered falsifying expense reports anything but irreprehensible. She is appalled by her actions and continues to beat herself up for her poor choices. She has also paid for them dearly.

On a gray, fall day in October 2009, Gillian reported to the equally dreary Federal Detention Center where she spent the next 18 months until she was released to a halfway house. On her way out the door, she was given a phone book to aid her in her job search and a half-hearted "good luck," as encouragement.

During her incarceration, Gillian worked in the prison kitchen and was eventually promoted to cleaning offices. She also found herself assisting inmates with their legal issues. But a lot of her mental energy was spent strategizing how she would mend her broken family and find employment once she was "out."

"I had this idea that I would be a valuable employee to defense attorneys. I had straddled both sides of the law and thought that I provided an interesting perspective that attorneys would find helpful. Boy, was I wrong. It was like I was radioactive. No one would get near me."

After numerous rejections from law firms, Gillian readjusted her expectations and began looking for lower skilled jobs. Right before Mother's Day she walked into a floral shop, and the owner, desperate for delivery drivers, hired her on the spot. Gillian enjoyed delivering flowers, but the job was seasonal and the pay unsustainable. She needed more stable employment. She set her sights on working as a stocking clerk for one of the larger grocery chains where she could count on steady work and health benefits.

The Safeway, near Gillian's home, was her prime target. Gillian did her research and found the name of a recruiter, Robin Lebeck, who she contacted with no results. As it happened, Gillian ran into Robin at a job fair. Since it was late in the day, the crowd had thinned out, and Robin invited Gillian to sit down.

"I spent at least 30 minutes talking to Robin," recalls Gillian. "I was very honest with her about my conviction, my contrition and my strong desire to get back to work and do whatever it takes to get my life back on track." Robin was positive about Gillian's chances of working at Safeway and agreed to set up a preliminary interview with a few decision makers.

Robin was true to her promise. Gillian did have interviews with a human resources specialist and a hiring manager. Both seemed to like her, and the feedback she got from Robin was that it was just a matter of moving some paperwork before she would get an offer. This was about the time I met Gillian. She mentioned in class that she was probably going to be working for Safeway soon and was very excited.

Over the next few months, I kept in touch with Gillian. Almost weekly, she called Robin to find out what was holding up the job offer and expressed her eagerness to start work. Each contact with Robin sounded promising, but the offer never materialized. Eventually, Robin avoided her calls and emails.

"Almost six months after the job fair, I was back to square one," said Gillian. "Although I did have a few 'pick up' jobs, such as handing out flyers for sporting events, I had put all my eggs in the Safeway basket and put my job search on hold. It was a big mistake."

Coincidently the leafleting gig led to a part-time food service job in the food court for a major sports team. Throughout the season, Gillian was guaranteed weekend employment. Grateful, for any paying job, she gave it her all, and her efforts did not go unnoticed. A supervisor from the restaurant company managing the food court invited her to apply for part-time work as a reservation hostess at one of their most popular restaurants.

This job was quite different than what Gillian was use to and often very hectic. Her customer service skills and ability to work under pressure were put to the test, and proved to be assets. Within a year she was promoted to the business office as a promotions assistant. She worked for the company for almost four-years until she was unexpectedly laid-off.

Being let-go was a blow to Gillian's ego. Although her employer explained that her position had changed and they were looking for someone more technically savvy, she couldn't help wonder if part of their decision had to do with her previous background. This time, Gillian found herself back in the job-finding game, in a better economy, with a new set of skills and a different last name (she had taken back her maiden name after her divorce was final). But she also had the same old insecurities. Would they find out about her background? Would she be marketable?

At first Gillian unsuccessfully applied to a variety of jobs postings online, many well beneath her skill level. As the end of her unemployment compensation drew near, she was feeling desperate and considered contract work. She signed up with several local staffing agencies that placed temporary workers in administrative jobs.

She quickly landed a temporary job as a contract specialist for a small technology firm where she is currently working. She reviews vendor contracts to ensure compliance with scope of work commitments. It is a job that pays a living wage and allows her to unpack her paralegal skills, which is an extra bonus. Since the company is facing a reorganization, she is not expecting to be hired as a full-time employee, but hopes her temporary contract will be extended as she is gaining valuable skills and experience that will eventually increase her marketability.

Gillian's life is not as she would have envisioned a decade ago, and her reentry into the job market has not been as quick or as permanent as she had hoped. But she views each employment experience as enriching and remains positive about her future. She is now ready to ratchet up her expectations where her career potential is concerned.

Side Note: Since meeting Gillian, I have trained her in the art of resume writing. For the last four years, she has come to my aid when my resume workload has been unmanageable, working on assignments during the evening or on weekends. She has grown into a skilled resume writer which has been a benefit to me and my clients.

Comments from Gillian:

When you first get out of prison, don't set your expectations too high. Be realistic about your skills and abilities and where they will fit into the marketplace. It may be worthwhile to meet with a career counselor at your state employment agency to get an objective view of your employment prospects. A career counselor can help you figure out how to transfer your skills to jobs and employers that are sympathetic to ex-offenders. As you gradually rebuild your resume, you can ratchet up your expectations and begin looking for more challenging work.

Instead of targeting the big name companies that often have inflexible hiring policies in place, approach smaller employers that aren't getting hundreds of resumes daily. They may be willing to bend the rules when they find good talent. Approach them face-to-face, and let them know of your desire to work for them. Don't expect to get hired overnight and don't let rejection slow you down. Jobs are out there if you are willing to put in the effort to find them.

Advice from Terry:
Don't wait around for a job offer.

A major flaw in Gillian's job search after her incarceration was assuming she had a job, before she had an offer. While waiting to hear back from Safeway, she put her job search on hold and wasted valuable time. After an interview, no matter how well you think it went, here are steps to take to ensure you keep moving your job search forward:

1. Evaluate your interview performance. What did you do well? What can you improve upon? Did you forget a key point you could include in your thank you note? Are there any responses to questions you need to practice for the next interview?

2. Write a persuasive thank you note. Don't make it bland or trite. Remind the employer of why he should hire you and leave him with a memorable example of your value. Let the interviewer know you want to work for the company and how you can make a contribution.

3. Apply for another job immediately after an interview, even if you are expecting a job offer the next day. Don't make the same mistake Gillian did and assume a good interview and positive feedback are promises of employment. Even if the hiring manager wants to hire you, there are many other factors at play. I have seen job offers made and rescinded because the hiring manager didn't know about an impending hiring freeze or a previous promise made to an internal candidate. In some cases, the company policy was inflexible and trumped the hiring manager's desire to hire a well-qualified candidate with a criminal backgrounds. Don't take rejection personally, but do apply for another job immediately. If you have a few irons in the fire, the rejection won't be quite as searing.

Apply for jobs that are a good fit.

When Gillian first got out of prison, she had unrealistic expectations regarding her job search. She mistakenly thought her paralegal certificate in combination with her real-world experience as a convicted felon would be an advantage to criminal law attorneys. Unfortunately, most law offices did not see it this way and Gillian lost valuable time in her job search.

She eventually found a temporary job in a flower shop and one with a food vendor. Although these jobs were below her skill level and in unfamiliar industries, she was successful rebuilding her work history and eventually worked her way into a full-time job in restaurant marketing.

When Gillian was laid-off after four-years of steady employment, her confidence was bruised and memories of her painful job search right out of prison were revived. Because she was feeling insecure and still clinging to that ex-offender mentality she applied for jobs well under her skill level, without success.

If employers are posting entry level jobs, they are looking for people with entry level skills who are willing to accept entry level salaries. If you are applying for jobs well below your skill and experience levels, most employers will not be interested in you for several reasons, even through their assumptions may be unfounded. For one, the salary will be lower than you are use to, so the employer assumes you will leave as soon as you can find a better job offer. For another, the employer may feel you won't be challenged in the job and will quickly get bored...and soon leave for another job.

Since Gillian had accrued an employment track record over the last four years, it was appropriate to set her sights a little higher than she had right after her incarceration. By agreeing to take on contract work, she is honing her paralegal skills and acquiring new skills that will continue to enhance her marketability.

Make the most of job fairs.

Don't expect to get a job offer at a job fair, but do attend them. Most employers participate as a public relations gesture, and very little hiring, if any, actually takes place. However, job fairs provide a great opportunity to network and learn about companies. Treat the job fair as you would an interview by dressing appropriately, having business cards and resumes available and your commercial or branding statement rehearsed.

When Gillian attended the job fair, she knew Safeway would be represented because she checked the participating employers in advance. As it turned out, Robin Labeck, the recruiter she had been trying to get a hold of unsuccessfully, was at the Safeway booth. It was the perfect opportunity for Gillian to introduce herself in person.

Because job fairs can be very crowded, go to the booths of the employers you most want to talk to first. When it is your turn to talk to the company representative, give a firm handshake, look the individual straight in the eye and recite your branding statement. Offer your resume and business card. Ask for the recruiter's business card in return, so you can contact her in the future.

Don't be shy about talking to the other job seekers standing in line with you. It is possible they are not looking for the same type of work or in the same location, but, like you, they have been out in the job market gathering information and may know of someone in your particular profession who is hiring. Likewise, offer information that may be helpful to others. What goes around, comes around.

What is the best time to attend a job fair? Most attendees arrive well before the doors open, mistakenly thinking first come, first hired. Since most employers don't hire at job fairs, the early birds are generally long forgotten by mid-morning. Since Gillian knew this, she arrived about an hour or so before the job fair was scheduled to end. By then, the lines had thinned out and the recruiters were more relaxed and able to spend more time with job seekers. Gillian spent almost a half-hour talking to Robin and established a comfortable relationships with her. Having met Gillian, Robin took time to thoroughly read her resume and was more responsive to Gillian's calls and emails. Robin set-up additional interviews at Safeway and served as her advocate. Although the job never panned-out, Gilian did not feel like an invisible job applicant and appreciated Robin's efforts on her behalf.

The Take-aways:

- ✓ Consult with an employment professional to help you identify your transferable skills and where they will be useful in the job market.
- ✓ Be realistic about how marketable you are in the current marketplace.
- ✓ Attend job fairs treating them as networking events.
- ✓ After a job interview, apply for another job.

Chapter 7
TONY S.
Take responsibility for your actions.
Don't be a victim.

"You cannot control what happens to you, but you can control your attitude toward what happens to you, and in that, you will be mastering change rather than allowing it to master you."

—Brian Tracy

Tony has always been an adaptable guy, which is what you would expect from an army brat who was born overseas and lived all over the world. Soft-spoken and personable, his ability to get along with others and adapt to change are his greatest strengths. They have also been his downfall.

Tony was born in Japan in the mid-1970s. His family eventually settled in California and then Washington where he graduated high school and went on to earn an associate degree in theology from Boise Bible College. Unsure about how he would use his education, he decided to join the U.S. Air Force, following in his father's footsteps. Three and a half years into his tour of duty, Tony received a non-combat injury and ended up in a hospital in Italy. By 2001, his military career was over and he moved to Portland, Oregon, to live with his brother. First he worked as a bartender to help pay the rent. Later, he got a day job at LensCrafters as a lab technician.

Music has always been an important part of Tony's life. Whether he was off duty in Riyadh, Saudi Arabia, lying in an Italian hospital or taking a bus to and from his jobs, he was always jotting down lyrics and new compositions to play on his guitar. Working in bars was a natural segue to picking up music gigs. Soon Tony was playing his original songs in local bars and coffee shops. During one of these performances he met Samantha, and his life changed dramatically.

It was Samantha who pursued Tony, first calling him at home and then showing up at his performances. True to Tony's easy-going nature, he passively went along with the relationship which advanced rapidly. Within a few months of their meeting, Samantha got pregnant and moved into her parent's home in Salt Lake City. She pressured Tony to join her, convincing him it would be easy to find work at another LensCrafters or similar establishment. Since relocating had never been a problem for Tony in the past, he felt sure he could find a job and reestablish his music career in Salt Lake City. Besides, with a child on the way, it was the right thing to do. Tony moved into Samantha's parent's home and shortly after they were married.

The changes in Tony's life were significant, but what he was least prepared for was the prevailing Mormon culture in Utah. In several job interviews, he was asked about his religious beliefs and church affiliations. The LensCrafter job never materialized. It was clear to Tony that if he wanted to support his family, he was going to have to join The Church. He did so for a brief time, but had difficulty embracing its beliefs.

By 2004, Tony knew he had to get out of Utah. He and Samantha, with their new baby, relocated to Portland, Oregon, where they both got jobs at a residential property leasing company. With two incomes, they started to build a comfortable life together. However, Tony was beginning to feel their life was too comfortable. They seemed to be acquiring material wealth at a rate that outpaced their earnings. When Tony finally realized Samantha was embezzling money from their employer, he quickly resigned, insisting Samantha do so as well. He relocated to Bellingham, Washington, in the hope that they would escape detection from their employer.

Tony quickly found a subsistence job at a K-Mart, and soon became estranged from his wife when he found out she was seeing another man. Demoralized, he drifted from one friend's house to another with very little purpose other than going to work and seeing his daughter as his work schedule and Samantha permitted.

It was on one of those father-daughter outings that Tony made an illegal turn and was stopped by a policeman. Because he wasn't getting his mail regularly, he was unaware that his former employer had accused him of embezzlement. He had missed a court date in Multnomah County, Oregon, and a warrant had been issued for his arrest.

Afraid for what might happen to his daughter if he implicated Samantha, Tony assumed full responsibility for the theft. He spent a total of eight months in Federal prison and a county correctional facility.

Upon Tony's release, he moved back to Washington state where a family member offered him housing. He began in earnest to build a career in music. He was successful finding music gigs on Craigslist and attended "open mike" nights to increase his visibility. He even recorded an album that he posted on MySpace. Its popularity helped advance his career. He appeared on a popular daytime television show as "local artist most likely to succeed" and on a widely viewed news magazine. Offers from wineries and similar venues materialized.

Tony also began working as a publicist to promote local bands and musicians. His talent for generating publicity expanded to the non-profit sector where to he promoted organizations such as Gilda's Club and the Arts Corps. Much of the work was volunteer. But he was earning enough to support himself while doing something he loved.

One would think that should be the end of a happy story, but a career in the entertainment industry is not an easy or reliable one. Tony had to constantly hustle to find his next job. He was also falling into an unhealthy lifestyle whereby late hours, alcohol, drugs and undependable friendships were difficult to avoid. Instead of continuing down this path, Tony decided to take control of his life. He was determined to find a healthier and more stable career.

Tony made two important decisions to facilitate his transition. The first was to make an appointment with a mental health counselor to help him restore his emotional health. Ever since his discharge from military service, he had been on auto pilot, falling into unhealthy relationships and feeling helpless to do anything about this. His doctor helped him realize that he did not have to be a victim. He had the personal power to take control of his life and determine its course.

The second decision was to visit the Department of Social and Human Services to explore job retraining opportunities. There he learned about the King County Job's Initiative (KCJI). With the promise of job retraining and employment assistance, he signed up for the job readiness training workshop, which is where I met Tony.

My first impression was of a sensitive young man with low confidence and high potential. An excellent writer with a knack for marketing, I tried to recruit and train him to be a career counselor, but after a few trial runs, we both agreed it wasn't the right fit for him.

Unfortunately, the promised funding for continuing education at a local community college fell through. Tony remained undaunted. Energized by his decision to find a new career, armed with job-finding tools from my workshop and encouraged by his KCJI case manager, Tony applied to a staffing agency for a contract job as a game tester for a large, but temporary project. There was a need for bodies, so background checks were lax and the work required very little specialized training. Although Tony was hired as a temporary employee at first, the agency was impressed by his professionalism and enthusiasm for the work. They continued to place him in similar jobs with increasing responsibility.

Soon Tony was supervising as many as 25 contracted game testers for a large software developer. He considered going back to school and earning a degree in software development in the gaming industry. He liked the work, appreciated a steady paycheck and was grateful for the structure it provided him.

However, Tony's life took another trajectory. One evening while walking back to his apartment, he was assaulted and seriously injured by a man on drugs. Tony's military training kicked in. By the time the police arrived, Tony had the perpetrator on the ground and a penknife to his throat. At first glance, the police could have mistaken Tony for the attacker. But Tony stayed calm and the police did not jump to conclusions. They asked clarifying questions of Tony, his assailant and eye-witnesses. Tony was treated with dignity and immediately taken to the hospital to be treated. Upon further questioning, Tony established a friendship with one of the officers. He developed new found respect for people working in law enforcement and, at the officer's suggestion, considered volunteering for the police department to promote its community education programs.

What this incident ultimately did for Tony, was bring him back to a vocation he loved, working with non-profits and artistic organization to promote their mission and services. He currently holds the title of Communications and Social Media Marketing Campaign Director for a non-profit financial services trade association. He has been busy promoting their mission and fund-raising events. When he is not promoting others, he is making music, his favorite job of all.

Comments from Tony:

Get out of prison mentally and stop thinking like a victim. Take responsibility for yourself and your actions, and ask for help in positive ways. Most likely you won't find the kind of help you need from family and friends. Go to social services organizations where you can get emotional, professional and financial support. And if you don't find it at the first door you knock on, keep trying until the right opportunities open up for you.

Advice from Terry:
Work with a staffing agency.

Staffing agencies help employers fill permanent, temporary and temp-to-hire jobs. They often advertise open positions on job boards without revealing the employer on whose behalf they are hiring. Tony got his game testing job by responding to a job posting from a staffing agency that had a contract with a large technology company to test its software products. Tony was considered a contract employee of the staffing agency through the length of the project, although he reported to work a the technology company's job site and performed as if he were one of the company's employees.

You should never pay a staffing agency to place you in a job. The employer pays the agency to fill a position and, in turn, the agency pays you a portion of that fee to do the job. There are many benefits to working with a staffing agency. If you are going to school or have other commitments and don't want to work full-time, you can accept temporary assignments. If you accept a temp-to-hire job, the employer has a chance to try you out, and you can decide if this is the employer you want to work for. If you have a bad experience with an employer, you can request that the agency put you in a different assignment. Having a contract or temporary project through a staffing agency is a good way to work for some prestigious employers that don't normally hire ex-offenders, and the experience will look good on your resume.

The down side to working with a staffing agency is that it gets a cut of your paycheck, and there are generally no additional benefits. (Although some agencies offer benefits, such as health care, if you have worked with them for a certain length of time.) Understandably, the agency has to make a profit to stay in business, but you don't want to work in a contract or temp-to-hire position for longer than three months if you are looking for full-time employment. If the employer is interested in hiring you as a full-time employee, he/she will want to wait until your contract with the staffing agency expires before putting you on the company payroll. Most employers will not buy out a contract with the staffing agency before it expires.

Before signing up with a staffing agency, ask if it hires people with "backgrounds." Many staffing agencies are franchised. Some franchise owners don't want the liability of hiring an ex-offender. Others won't see it as a problem, especially if they are hiring for construction labor and other trade positions. Two staffing agencies with the same name, in different locations, may have different owners, and very different hiring policies.

Volunteer to expand your network and experience

Throughout his career, Tony did a tremendous amount of volunteer work, usually in the form of getting free publicity for bands, community events and non-profit organizations. Through volunteering, Tony was connecting to organizations who had influential supporters. His volunteer work with a non-profit that supports services for foster children helped connect him to his current employer. It is a perfect example of paying it forward.

Many people think volunteering is "working for free," a concept that seems counterintuitive when you are looking for paid employment. Yes, you are working for no monetary gain, but the volunteer experience can be as minimal as a one-time event or just a few hours a month and has numerous rewards, such as:

- Learning new skills and gaining new experiences to enhance your marketability.
- Expanding your professional network. Most people who volunteer are active in their communities and have a large network you can tap into.
- Developing your references. The volunteer coordinator or other staff associated with the organization you volunteer for will be grateful for your help and willing to serve as employment references.
- Filling a gap in your resume. If your job search is taking longer than expected, having a volunteer job will be a good way to fill in a work gap. It doesn't matter if you didn't get paid for your work, as long as you performed a service.

You can find volunteer opportunities on your local United Way website or through a website called VolunteerMatch.org. Although some organizations that work with vulnerable populations will require a background check, many do not. Pick your volunteer opportunities strategically. They should be compatible with your career objectives, have lots of networking opportunities and involve a cause you are interested in or care about.

Build a portfolio career.

What I admire most about Tony is the courage he had to walk away from the things he loved, but instinctively knew were not good for him. He turned away from a toxic marriage, despite the pain of not seeing his daughter, and he left a career in music when it started turning destructive. It takes great self awareness and bravery to take control of your life, to forsake comfortable but bad habits or take the easy way out.

After grounding himself in a survival job as a game tester, Tony was gradually able to return to some of the things he loved—his music, putting together special events and promoting causes he cared about. He was building a portfolio career that capitalized on his skills and interests.

A portfolio career is made up of multiple part-time or temporary jobs in one or several professions. While Tony was employed as a game tester, he was also working as a publicist for a non-profit related to disadvantaged children, and still picking up music gigs here and there.

The advantage of having a portfolio career is that it offers flexibility, variety, and in many cases a better work/life balance. Some people find that having a portfolio career allows them to participate in their many and diverse interests, like the warehouse worker who runs a commercial photography business on the weekends. For most, the portfolio career is appealing in that you are in control of your own fate, not dependant on the whim of an employer for financial security.

On the flip side, portfolio careers require a great deal of self-discipline and superior time management skills as you are often juggling multiple and diverse projects simultaneously. Some portfolio careerist report feeling isolated and anxious regarding the lack of guaranteed income. Networking and marketing are also critical components to keeping your name in the public eye and the jobs coming in, but are not always popular tasks, especially for the introverted. The reality is most portfolio careers come without healthcare benefits or paid vacation and sick leave although there are those rare employers who may provide benefits to contractors and part-timers after having worked a certain number of hours.

These are all important factors to think about when considering multiple employment, especially if you have a low tolerance for risk. If the idea of multiple income streams is appealing to you, here are some helpful tips:

- Identify your skills and interests that are most in demand in industries that are expanding.
- Brainstorm a variety of potential income streams and determine which are most viable. They should vary in their complexity and risk. You want at least one job that isn't too taxing but will bring in steady income.
- Look for every opportunity to build on and expand your network.
- Consider writing articles for publication, blogging or public speaker to create a platform to market yourself.
- Start out slowly. Keep your day job and try moonlighting at first. Gradually expand your projects and options until you feel emotionally and financially ready to say good-bye to traditional employment.

The Take-aways:

- ✓ Don't be an emotional prisoner. Take charge of your life and walk away from unhealthy situations.
- ✓ Get out into the community and volunteer to do work you love. You will be doing something you enjoy and eventually the connections will pay off.
- ✓ If you have multiple interests and want untraditional employment, consider a portfolio career.

Chapter 8
ROGER N.
Turning fortunate accidents into opportunities.

"We do not create our destiny; we participate in its unfolding. Synchronicity works as a catalyst toward the working out of that destiny."
—David Richo

Roger is loyal to a fault. This may explain why he was laid off three times during his senior-level career in marketing and graphic design with large engineering companies in Michigan. "I always went down with the ship," he said referring to employers who were either acquired by larger companies or closed for financial reasons. In most cases, Roger was able to rebound by using his contacts to land his next position. But in 2005, at age 54, he lost more than a job.

His children were now grown and living on their own. His 25-year marriage was ending. Between 2005 and 2007, he struggled to find a job in the worst economy in decades, and Michigan was especially hard hit. Both his house and his car were in jeopardy. That's when depression set in. Seldom a drinker, Roger let his guard down, as well as his better judgment. After a day of networking that included beer and tequila, he extended his activities into the evening, was caught for speeding and slapped with a DUI.

It was also a wake-up call. Roger knew he needed to get back in control of his life. After working with a career counselor and doing some serious introspection, he kept returning to a long time dream of teaching fine arts at a community college. While he was raising a family, the profession wasn't sustainable. Competition for these jobs was fierce and the pay was inadequate, so he continued to drift back to the business world. Now his situation was different. He was accountable for only himself. Perhaps it was time to explore a teaching job in a purposeful way. But first, Roger set out on a journey to reconnect with his friends and acquaintances.

In 2007 Roger traveled to Minneapolis, Chicago, Albuquerque and Denver. In Seattle, he saw an ad in an art magazine for a degree program for leadership in the fine arts at Seattle University. This seemed like the kind of career match he was looking for.

"I call it, the power of synchronicity," said Roger. "With this kind of degree I could combine my leadership skills with my fine arts background to help bring fine arts into the public domain. My plan was to complete the certificate and return to Michigan to work as a consultant for public arts programs."

Roger settled into life in Seattle with a career goal in mind and a list of resources to pursue it. Through student loans and his 401K, he was able to fund his education. He also received treatment for his depression at a community clinic. It was during a spontaneous visit to the Mayor's Office for Senior Citizens that he learned about and applied for a state sponsored internship. He was accepted and began working as a part-time administrative assistant for the WorkSource Center (Washington state's one-stop employment service) at a local community college.

Upon graduating with a Master in Fine Arts for Arts Leadership, Roger moved back to Michigan to pursue consulting work. He wanted to use his degree to help small towns and cities develop their public arts programs. But the lone wolf nature of consulting no longer appealed and the idea of teaching still niggled him. Since he had established strong ties in Seattle and had enjoyed his internship at the community college, he decided to return to the Puget Sound and continue to explore opportunities.

Back in Seattle, Roger became very involved in the fine and performing arts community and participated on several advisor boards and volunteer projects. Through his contacts with public agencies and a carefully established network, he applied for a few positions at the local community college where he had previously completed his internship. Impressed by his performance, the school hired Roger as a part-time instructor and part-time employment specialist teaching business, technology and career development classes. Not exactly what he envisioned, but it was another step in his quest for satisfying employment.

As he suspected, Roger loved teaching and, with a little bit of innovative thinking, he was able to integrate his background in the fine arts into his curriculum, whether he was teaching math, technical writing or job search skills. He has also managed to parlay his talents as a commercial artist into several public exhibitions of his work. In a way, Roger has come full-circle. He is now living what was a seed of an idea while working in the corporate world. Being open to possibilities and methodically following though brought Roger's career vision to fruition.

Comments from Roger:

I am a strong believer in synchronicity. But it is also up to us to make these fortunate accidents come together by developing an awareness of the signs along life's way. Open your eyes, and really look at what is happening around you. Then, come up with a plan and act on it. Keep moving forward by being open to and using the resources at your disposal. Then pause, take some time to assess, recalibrate and apply new strategies. Making a life change doesn't happen all at once. It comes in small increments that continually need fine-tuning. You also need to be nimble enough to recognize when opportunities do appear and react quickly to the possibilities.

Advice from Terry:

Stay open to new possibilities.

When I first met Roger, he was struggling with many employment barriers. He was an unemployed *mature worker* (a label given to people over age 50) and living in a new community during a difficult economy. He was overcoming issues related to depression and trying to figure out how he would apply his recently acquired education into sustainable employment.

What impressed me, was how Roger quickly established roots in the arts and academic communities in Seattle. This was partially through his internship, volunteer work, networking savvy and willingness to embrace social service programs.

More significant is the way Roger took a position as a business instructor and employment specialist (jobs not exactly thought of as artistic) and molded them into what is close to being his dream job. He clearly had the business acumen to perform this job from years of working in the private sector. But he also used his creativity to integrate his artistic, right-brain temperament and fine arts background into a very left-brain curriculum. The classroom teaching and one-on-one counseling his job required were also job functions that he always want to try and, having done so, found them immensely rewarding.

Never stop learning.

Roger was already a well educated individual, but he took advantage of every learning opportunity that would help him advance personally and professionally, from getting a Masters in Fine Arts to taking my job finding skills training class. He realized the old adage that "knowledge is power" and actively looked for opportunities get more education to enhance his current skills and future career interests.

In today's job market, if you don't have a GED (General Education Development) certificate, you are at a serious disadvantage. Almost all employers require a high school diploma or GED as a minimum educational requirement. Many correctional facilities offer GED programs. If you are reading this book while incarcerated and don't have a GED, seriously consider using this opportunity to get one. It will make you more marketable upon release and allow you talk about how you have been productive during your incarceration.

Community colleges and state employment centers can also assist you in finding a GED program. There are many online programs that can prepare you for the GED exam such as GEDforFree.com.

Advice for the mature worker.

Like Randy, many of the students that attend my class are over 40 and are considered "protected workers" according to the Age Discrimination employment act of 1967. Although it is illegal to discriminate against older workers, this practice does exist, but is difficult to prove. Being a "mature worker with a record" adds additional complexity to the job search. Here are some suggestion for overcoming ageism and demonstrating your value in the workplace.

Create an age neutral resume.

In the same way a well-written resume should not reveal your status as an ex-offender, it should also conceal your age. Career counselors recommend leaving dates off education after five years. You can indicate that you graduated high school, but you don't have to tell the employer it was in 1982. It is also recommended that you provide only the last 10—15 years of employment on your resume. This is often a problem for ex-offenders who tend to have large gaps in their work history. Consider creating a skills-based or functional resume—a good way to hide dates that are ancient history.

Update your wardrobe.

You don't need to dress like a teenager nor should you look like a grandparent. Being well groomed and fashionably dressed will give the appearance of youth and professionalism. Many agencies, such as Goodwill Industries, provide interview clothing and fashion advice to job seekers of all ages. If your are overweight, try to shed a few pounds (another factor related to job discrimination). Should you dye the gray hair? I leave that up to you.

Show enthusiasm and energy.

One of the myths that exists about older workers is that they no longer have the energy to produce at the same levels as younger workers. Many studies conducted by AARP prove that the older worker is just as productive, if not more so, than their younger counterparts. A nice smile and display of enthusiasm will counteract the wrinkles and age spots.

Evaluate and update your skills.

The reality is that as you get older it is harder to perform in physically demanding jobs. You may need to retrain for jobs that are less physical or update your skills to compete with new workers entering your field. AARP offers worker retraining programs and computer class as do most state employment centers.

Show your value.

Prepare stories of what you have done in the past to bring value to your employer. How did you make money, save money, improve safety or train other employees on the job? This is what the employer really cares about. If you can demonstrate your worth, you will be a valuable commodity, no matter how old you are.

The Take-aways:

- ✓ Take advantage of your network and community resources
- ✓ Stay open to new opportunities
- ✓ Advance your education whenever you can
- ✓ Don't let age get in the way of your job search

Chapter 9
ANNA F.
To make positive changes, get to know yourself.

"Persistence and resilience only come from having been given the chance to work though difficult problems."

—Gever Tulley

Anna was born and educated in the Soviet Union. She earned a master's degree in bilingual education and was building a successful career teaching Russian as a second language to international students. It was the mid-1980s, and the Soviet Union was in turmoil politically and economically. So was Anna's home life. Against her better judgment, Anna agreed to a marriage arranged by her parents. The union showed signs of trouble from the start. Her new husband, Pavel, was narcissistic and controlling. Anna hoped that she could change these negative tendencies, especially with the birth of two children.

In the early 1990s, because of her husband's activities, Anna and Pavel were forced to leave Moscow as political refugees. Disheartened to leave family and friends, Anna decided to embrace her move to the United States and considered it a fresh start for her marriage. Her husband relocated the family to a remote community in Western Washington where he started an import business. At first, the business flourished, and Pavel refused to let Anna work. The isolation she felt was overwhelming. But as the economy began to weaken, so did Pavel's business concerns. By 2001 the family was on welfare, and Anna knew she needed to find a job.

Anna was hired as a program coordinator for a nonprofit that provided adult basic education programs. She loved serving others and was energized by her work. But life at home was difficult. No longer the sole bread-winner,

Pavel suffered from low self-esteem and took his frustrations out on the family, verbally and physically. He began to show up at Anna's work to check on her. Anna did her best to keep her personal problems hidden from her coworkers, but more than once, she called the community hotline for help when trouble started at home. Anna knew she had to end the marriage. She just didn't know how. She feared for her safety and the well-being of her children.

In 2005, Pavel decided he had enough of the United States. He left for Europe intending to send for the family as soon as he found work. In the meantime, Anna had been promoted to a management position within her agency. In Pavel's absence, life at home was calmer. But the anticipation of Pavel's return and an inevitable confrontation left her on edge. Anna began gambling. This quickly became an escape from her anxieties. (She was later diagnosed with post traumatic stress disorder.) The habit took on a life of its own, and Anna began "borrowing" money from the organization where she worked. In 2010, she pleaded guilty to embezzlement and served a month of house arrest.

The humiliation Anna felt was bad, but the loss of the work she loved was more devastating. For several months after her conviction, she felt paralyzed to action. Not only was she ashamed to go out in public, but the threat of Pavel's return was ever present.

Anna started seeing a mental health counselor for her depression and anxiety, but it was the Internet that helped restore her confidence and self-esteem. Visiting chat rooms, she discovered that there were other men and women like her who had been in similar situations and had made positive changes in their lives. She began asking herself difficult questions such as, "Who am I?" "How do I want to change?" "Can I make that change happen?" After much introspection, Anna realized she could change her way of thinking. She did not have to be labeled a criminal for the rest of her life. She still remembers one message from an ex-felon who was now a manager of a successful computer store. It resonated with her. "Ask for help," he said.

Finding the right kind of help wasn't as easy as Anna had hoped. Many social service agencies are not well-integrated. Their services are fragmented and eligibility is often narrowly defined and restrictive. In a few cases, the case manager she was assigned to was not a good fit for her circumstances. There were a few false starts and many set-backs, but Anna refused to be discouraged. She remained true to her job search and commitment to asking for help.

Eventually, by networking with various county program coordinators and participants, Anna found the King County Jobs Initiative. With the enthusiastic support of Trisha, her case manager, Anna no longer felt unemployable. Armed with job finding strategies from my job readiness training workshop and Trisha's encouragement, Anna was almost ready to look for work. But first, she needed a place to live, in a new community where past connections and memories would not conjure bad feelings and erode her confidence—and where Pavel couldn't find her.

Anna considered moving into a women's shelter in another county, close to her now-adult children. One afternoon when she was in her car exploring, she took a wrong turn. As she started to turn around, she noticed a sign that read "Kingdom of Hope, Christian Transitional Housing for Women." Anna was drawn to the facility. When she went inside, it was as if the executive director had been expecting her. She was greeted warmly and interviewed on the spot. Within two days Anna had a new home for the next two years, where she could experience the safety, stability and spiritual support this new community of 14 women provided.

With her basic needs taken care of, Anna started her job search with determination. Trisha sent her job leads that she immediately followed up on. She also continued to network whenever possible. Unfortunately, she was also up against an economic recession and her search for employment was taking much longer than she had hoped.

One contact who proved most helpful was Roger N., featured in the previous chapter of this book. Now a part-time employment specialist and part-time instructor, I suggested Anna network with Roger, and she took the initiative to do so. He helped Anna to customize her resume for different jobs in nonprofit agencies. He encouraged her to check out employer websites rather than waiting passively for job openings. One nonprofit agency that appealed to Anna was a faith-based human services organization that depended largely on volunteer power to advance its mission. In her research, she discovered that the organization was started by a family who had a history of working in prisons, retraining inmates and creating jobs opportunities for them upon release.

Now that Anna had a clear focus, a list of specific employers that may be sympathetic to her background and a resume that showed she had the related job skills being advertised, her job search began realizing results. In one week she had three job interviews, and with Trisha's positive reference, a job offer followed soon after. Anna was employed by the faith-based organized she was originally drawn to. She assumed an administrative role, working with the agency's large volunteer base. Today she is able to contribute her personnel and organizational skills to make a difference in the lives of others. In turn, the work has nurtured her spirituality and self-confidence, allowing her to grown professionally and feel like a valuable contributor to her community.

Comments from Anna:

Take the time to ask, "Who am I?" and "How do I want to change?" If you are sincere about wanting to make a change, develop a plan to move on and don't be afraid to ask others for help.

Indentify who you want to work for and who will want you as an employee. After doing some careful research, I knew my current employer would be a perfect fit, based on the organizations missions and values. With determination, and a little help from my case manager, I pursued my target agency and hit a bulls eye.

Network, network, network. Friends (and often strangers) will be your lifeline for finding the resources, training or employers who can make the change you desire possible. They will also serve as credible sources when an employer asks for your references.

Advice from Terry:

Identify the employers you want to work for.

With Roger's advice, Anna was no longer thoughtlessly sending out resumes. He helped her develop a methodical job search. Instead of spending hours on the computer applying for jobs that may already have been filled or were non-existent, she allocated her time to researching companies. Then she made a list of companies who had missions and values that were compatible with her own and began networking to find connections that could help her get in the door.

When making your target employer list (I often refer to this as your marketing plan), strive to identify 20 to 60 employers you could work for. To be practical, look for employers who are closest to home first. It is also more efficient to group your lists by industry or product classification. For example, if you are looking for a delivery driver job you might divide your targets into furniture, food or appliances. Your marketing plan would look something like this:

MY MARKETING PLAN

Career Objective: Delivery Driver

Job Related Skills/Qualifications: Two years experience; safe driving record; CDL-A

Criteria: Within 10 miles from home, accessible by bus

Potential Employers:

Furniture:	Food:	Appliances:
Sears	Charlie's Produce	Albert's Appliances
Macy's	Amazon Fresh	King Appliances
Greenfield Furniture	Roberto's Pizza	Maytag
IKEA	Kroger's Home Delivery	Kenmore

Your marketing plan will help you stay focused, and your job search will be more efficient. A good resource to help you make your target employer list is an old fashion phone book. If you don't have one at home, you can get one at the library. Phone books list employers by category and geographically. Online phone directories and local Chamber of Commerce directories will also help you identify employers close to your home.

Make networking your top priority.

A 2014 study by CareerXroads showed that only 15 percent of jobs were filled from job boards. Most jobs were filled internally or through referrals. More than 70 percent of job hunters found their jobs through networking. This included meeting with friends and acquaintances, attending trade and association meetings or volunteering.8

Whether it was her counselors, members of online chat rooms or employment specialists like Trisha and Roger, Anna recognized the value of these relationships and cleverly established a network for emotional support as well as help with her job search. Her network was also a ready source for job references.

If you are like many ex-offenders who have been out of circulation for months or years, you probably have a very small group of contacts and sparse list of references. Inviting case managers, teachers, clergy and other professionals into your network is a start. In her book, *A Foot in the Door: Networking Your Way into the Hidden Job Market,* Katharine Hansen lists the top 50 networking hot spots. Here are the top 10:

- Professional organizations, trade associations and labor unions
- Volunteer organizations
- Charity and fundraising events
- Civic and community groups
- Religious community

8 "Don't Believe These 8 Job Search Myths," Hannah Morgan, U.S. News & World Report, Spet. 17, 2014

- Golf course
- Tennis, squash, racquetball, basketball court
- Health club, spa, YMCA
- Political campaign
- Chamber of commerce

The social media is also a good way to network without leaving the comfort of your home. Facebook is an easy way to quickly develop a network and let people in on your job search. But be sure to keep your photos and comments professional. A better tool for online networking while job hunting is LinkedIn. Similar to Facebook, this is a social network used by professionals. The best way to distinguish these social media tools is to think of Facebook as your family room and LinkedIn as your office. LinkedIn allows you to download your resume for others to see, find people who may be connected to your target companies, participate in group discussions and receive job postings. After receiving your resume, many recruiters and hiring managers will cross-reference you on LinkedIn. So it is important to keep your LinkedIn profile up-to-date and career focused.

How to manage a long job search.

Each job seeker has a unique set of circumstances that impact the speed and quality of the job search, but all agree extended unemployment can be demoralizing, if not paralyzing. In Anna's case, she needed to regain her self-esteem, find housing and take time to consider her options. This didn't happen right away. Once she began looking for work, the economy was in recession and the responses to her job search efforts were disappointing. It seemed as if her life was destined to be one long job search.

If finding a job is taking longer than you expected, here are a few additional suggestions to keeping your job search momentum:

Treat you job search as a full-time job.

It is true that the more effort you put into your job search, the faster the pay-off. If you can't devote at least six hours a day on a job search, at least try to do something every day. A phone call, a meeting, a job application is one step closer to employment and better than doing nothing.

Join a job support group or find a job buddy.

Whether virtual, by phone or face-to-face, a job club will make you feel more committed to your job search, less isolated and can generate leads. Try to meet with your job support group weekly. You can find these groups by looking online, through your state's employment agency or often at a place of worship. If you can't find a group to join, try to find a job search buddy. Agree to check in with each other at least once a week by phone or over coffee to discuss the week's challenges and accomplishments. When you have a job search buddy you will feel less alone and more accountable to meet your job search goals.

Celebrate the little successes.

Treat yourself to a walk after submitting a resume. Buy yourself a latte after an interview. Set small goals and reward yourself when you achieve them.

Don't take rejection personally.

There are many reasons for not getting a job. Internal job candidates, hiring freezes, or a highly competitive job market are just a few. Remind yourself that each rejection is a step closer to the job that is meant for you. The job search is, in part, a numbers game. If you play the odds, you will eventually wind up a winner.

The Take-aways:

✓ Change the way you think about yourself. Identify your positives and don't dwell on the negatives.

✓ Select the employers you want to work for. Research them carefully to make sure they are compatible with your values and employment needs...and will hire people with your background.

✓ Look for ways to network physically and through social media channels.

✓ Don't get discouraged if your job search takes longer than you planned.

✓ Find a job search buddy or join a job club.

Chapter 10
GRIF M.
Your attitude is everything.

"Once you replace negative thoughts with positive ones, you have positive results."

—Willie Nelson

You can't help but smile when you meet Grif. His ebullient personality is infectious. When I first met this middle-aged, African American man in my job readiness class, I found his radiant smile and colorful rap captivating. I would let him talk on and on, forgetting I had a class to conduct. But Grif also had a darker side that erupted on occasion, and he was not inhibited about expressing his fears. In prison he had a steady job, shelter, three-square meals and a routine—with no surprises. He was well liked by guards and inmates alike. He also had a reputation as an accomplished drummer. Not only did he perform, he also taught others.

Having been incarcerated for more than ten years, being on the "outside" was a daunting prospect. Would he find employment? Would he find housing? Would he be tempted to slip back into old habits and reoffend? Freedom held promise and peril. Was he up to the challenge?

Grif grew up in Baltimore and enlisted in the United States Navy in the early 1980s. He was trained as an aircraft mechanic. After completing military service with a honorable discharge, he returned to Baltimore and attended a technical school to become an automotive technician. He had mechanical acumen, a good job and a promising future—until he became addicted to cocaine.

Thinking he could break his habit if he left Baltimore and his toxic friends, Grif moved around the country and ended up in Washington state. Being a skilled mechanic, it wasn't hard for him to find work, but it seemed impossible for him to stay away from drugs. By the early 1990s, Grif had lost all direction and started robbing banks to support his habit. His first incarceration cost him nine months in Sheridan, Illinois; his second, 41 months in Florence, Colorado; and his third, nine years in Texas and California. Grif was well-traveled, but saw little of the real world.

In February 2014, Grif was released to a halfway house. He had two goals. Find work and find lodging. Every day for two months he went to his local one-stop employement center and he wasn't shy about asking for help. He took classes to develop previously non-existent computer skills. He also got into a counseling program for Veterans. There he was connected to the King County Jobs Initiative.

When I walked into the classroom on an unexpectedly sunny April morning, I was prepared to cancel class when it looked like only four students would be attending, two short of my minimum requirement. But Grif was so eager for the knowledge he knew would help him find a job, his enthusiasm had already infected the three fellow classmates. It was clear I couldn't send these fellows home and call it a day. It was class as usual.

During the second day of class, Grif got an invitation to interview for a sales associate position in the drum department of a large music chain. Quick to take my advice about researching employers, he immediately got online and started gathering information on the company and memorizing the employee profiles that were posted on the site. He studied up on the manufacturer of drums and accessories. He was psyched and extremely well-prepared for the interview.

I contacted Grif the following week to see how the meeting went, hoping he had received a job offer.

"I believe the interview went well," he said. "I'm sure they liked me, but after looking around the store, I don't think I was a good fit with the clientele. They didn't seem like my kind of people. They weren't customers I could relate to and visa versa."

When I asked if the interviewer inquired about his record, Grif became agitated. "Yes, he did. And this is the problem I am still struggling with. I get mad when someone asks me about my background. It is hard to hide my anger because it is none of their business."

Unfortunately, Grif was wrong on this point. The employer has every right to ask about past convictions. Although Grif was prepared with a reasonable answer, his delivery showed his annoyance. With a pep talk and some practice, he was ready to take on the next interviewer who might pry into his past.

A few days later, Grif was contacted by a large home improvement chain for a warehouse position. He had made his original contact at a job fair and was later referred by a store employee. With a little more practice on those annoying interview questions and a lot of positive thinking, Grif impressed the hiring manager. A few days after the interview, he received an offer to work the graveyard shift.

Within a few weeks, Grif moved out of the halfway house and into his own room in a multi-residential house on a quiet street in east Seattle. Within three month, he was putting in substantial overtime and recognized as an Employee of the Month.

Back in the workforce, Grif, was still getting use to his newly found freedom which was becoming less intimidating with each day. Step by step he was starting to build a savings account and make plans for his future beyond bars.

Side Note: When I last heard from Grif, he had left the warehouse job and joined the union as a welding apprentice. He was making a union wage, had moved in to a house with his lady friend and just purchased a previously owned Mustang.

Comments from Grif:

No matter how frustrated you get by the interview questions that get thrown at you, accept it as a step in the process you have to go through. Practice your response to those difficult questions and think positive. Your attitude is everything, so exercise, pray and seek advice from people you trust.

Advice from Terry:

Update your computer skills.

Having been incarcerated for ten years, one of the first hurdles Grif had to overcome was learning how to use a computer and other technology that did not exist a decade ago. While most of us take computers and smart phones for granted, individuals who have been incarcerated for long periods of time don't have access to technology and are at a disadvantage. Grif immediately recognized this skill deficit and quickly found a resource where he could get a free cell phone. For the next few months his living situation would be in transition. Having a cell phone meant he would be accessible to employers no matter where he slept.

Next, he knew he needed to take some classes to gain computer skills. Grif signed up at the state one-stop employment center for free classes. He learned the basics such as conducting research on the Internet, responding to online job applications, and creating a Word document to develop his resume and attach it to an email message. Libraries, community colleges and social service agencies, such as Goodwill and the Salvation Army, are great (and generally free) places to learn the basic computer skills that are a mandatory requirement for finding a job in today's marketplace.

Most correctional facilities in the country are sorely lacking in resources to prepare its inmate population to find jobs upon release. Grif sought out all the resources available to him including those offered by the Veteran Administration. At the state employment center, he learned about my job readiness training class. Because he had been out of circulation for a decade, he knew that finding a job was not the same today as it was before his incarceration and immediately enrolled in my class. In addition to computer skills, he needed information on how to negotiate today's job market. A quick study, it didn't take Grif long to apply what he learned. He was employed within four weeks of completing my workshop.

Prepare a script to discuss your conviction.

Grif is the type of person who wears his emotions on his sleeve, which has its advantages and disadvantages. It was important for him to get those face-to-face meetings with employers so they could experience first-hand his energy and enthusiasm. However, when the interviewer asked questions that Grif found irrelevant or intrusive, his annoyance was clearly apparent and off-putting. Once Grif was comfortable with his responses to questions about his background, he could relax and accept the process, even if he didn't like it.

Responding to unpleasant questions makes most job candidates uncomfortable. *Have you ever been fired from a job? Why were you out of work for so long? Did you ever have a disagreement with a boss or coworker? How do I know I can trust you?* These are the frequently asked interview questions that make most job hunters cringe. That is why it is so important to prepare and practice your responses in advance of an interview. Think about delivering a short, direct response to the question and then bridge to the positive. End your script with what you learned from the experience or what you have done to improve your personal and professional development. Practice with a career coach or a trusted friend. And, like Grif, think positive.

Here is an example of a script that you can adapt to your situation.

"I have two things I need to tell you before we complete this interview. The first, is that I may not pass the background check. Several years ago I started hanging around with a bad crowd and made some poor choices. I became addicted to drugs and held up a bank to support my habit.

During my time in a correctional facility, I earned my GED, took classes on improving my interpersonal relationships and faithfully attended AA meetings. I have been clean and sober for more than a year and have a new and very supportive group of friends.

The second thing you should know is that I really want to work for your company and am committed to doing whatever it takes to prove my worth and make a substantial contribution. I am hoping you will give me that chance."

Practice positive self-talk.

Affirmations refer to the practice of positive thinking and self-empowerment. There is a school of thinking that if you write down positive statements and repeat them to yourself each day, they will become imbedded in your sub-conscious. Eventually, you will act on these subconscious thoughts and they will be come reality. We do know negative self-talk can be damaging. Whether affirmations work or not, it is better for your psyche to choose positive words over the negative concerning your situation.

Whenever Grif caught himself thinking that he was not good enough to get a job, that he lacked inner-strength and was going to fail, he had enough self-awareness to realize what he was doing. He made a conscious effort to turn those thoughts around to, "I know I will get a job. I know someone will want to hire me. I know I will be an outstanding employee."

Just saying these affirming statements out loud brought a smile to Grif's face and new energy to his body language. It is a habit he now practices daily.

If you want to try the power of positive thinking, here are some tips to keep in mind. Keep your affirming statements short and use positive language. Relax as you say them. Repeat them a couple of times each day. Here are few examples of common affirmations:

- I am a good father (or mother, husband, wife)
- I am happy, healthy and strong of mind and body.

- Good things will come my way.
- I am a hard worker and have a lot to offer.
- I am employable.
- I have many marketable skills.

The Take-aways:

- ✓ Update your computer and job finding skills.
- ✓ Prepare your script and practice talking about the difficult questions with people you trust, before an interview.
- ✓ Freedom can be scary. Avoid negative self-talk and stay positive.

Chapter 11
MICHAEL B.
Do what you love.

"Your work is going to fill a large part of your life, and the only way to be truly satisfied is to do what you believe is great work. And the only way to do great work is to love what you do."
—Steve Jobs

Growing up in Seattle's Central District, Michael was white minority in a multi-racial community. He lived with his single mother and two older sisters. His father, a rock musician of some notoriety, committed suicide a few months before Michael was born.

A straight A student and talented musicians, Michael could play guitar, drums, bass and several other instruments. He did have a small group of friends, but he was often bullied and got into fights. It wasn't an easy life for this sensitive, highly impressionable young man without a father figure he could turn to.

Prior to Michael starting fourth grade, his mom moved the family to a suburban community southeast of Seattle. For the next two years, he continued to make good grades and practice his music. But the bullying continued and he felt angry all the time.

In middle school, Michael fell in with a more accepting group of friends. It improved his self-esteem among his peers, but had a negative impact on his academic life. By sixth grade, he was skipping school to hang out with his friends, mostly smoking marijuana and drinking alcohol. His first visit to the "Juvie Center" was age 14, when he was caught trespassing and causing a ruckus while riding his dirt bike on private property.

A hard worker when motivated, Michael got his first job when he was 15. Jeannie, his oldest sister, was working for a large property management company and got her younger brother a job assisting the property maintenance team. Michael enjoyed painting, using tools and fixing things, but what he enjoyed most was the money he earned. Most of it was reinvested in drugs and alcohol.

No longer willing to attend public school, Michael tried home schooling in 7th and 8th grade, but by 9th grade he dropped out. He worked a series of jobs, such as landscaping and auto detailing, as a means to support his cocaine habit.

Late one snowy night while out drinking, Michael and his friends stole a pick up truck and then an ATV quad which fit nicely in the truck's cab. Both had high resell value. Before they were out of the neighborhood, the police were on their tail and they were in a high speed chase through the snow-covered suburban streets.

Eventually, their truck popped its tires when they drove over a spike strip laid down by the police. Michael and his friends abandoned the truck and ran. With only a sweatshirt to keep him warm, Michael crouched in the bushes in someone's backyard. A few blocks away he could hear dogs barking and the police shouting. He knew his friends had been caught. Michael continued to hide until it got quiet.

"It was like watching myself in a movie, so surreal," said Michael. "The fear and adrenaline were pumping through me. Then things got really crazy."

Too cold to stay hidden much longer, Michael ventured out into the cold, dark night directly into a cadre of policeman who expeditiously had him down on the ground and handcuffed.

With two-felonies on his record, (one for the truck and the other for the ATV) Michael spent four months of a six-month sentence in a county jail. Although he worried a lot about being sent to a federal prison, it never happened. In jail he became a trustee and worked in the kitchen. Upon his release he was drug-free and ready to make better choices.

Like most drug users, Michael's good intentions were replaced by bad habits. "I still had a victim mentality. I continued to blame others for the bad hand I was dealt. My family was disgusted with me, and I was weak and unwilling to take accountability for myself."

Shortly after his release, Michael became addicted to oxycontin, a powerful prescription drug. Then he started snorting heroin. Soon he was stealing from family members and friends to pay for drugs. Angry and tremendously disappointed, his family kicked him out of the house. He spent most of his time on the streets strung out on heroin or methamphetamines. Michael had been a serious drug addict for three years.

In 2014, Carl, an old elementary school friend got in touch with Michael. He was living in Farmerville, Texas, and encouraged Michael to move in with him. Carl convinced Michael that he needed to get a way from bad influences and the change would do him good. What Michael didn't know was that Carl was not clean. After he moved to Texas, his addiction got worse and he became an IV user. Michael found himself drifting in and out of psychosis for long periods of time.

"One night I went to a strip club in Dallas and literally got lost for a week. For seven days, I just walked and walked, often in circles drifting in and out of reality. I don't know if I ate or slept. I must have finally asked someone for directions, but honestly, I don't really know how I got back home."

Looking back, Michael said he found this period of his life spiritually humbling and a cry for help. He just didn't know how to get it. All he knew was that he had to get back to Washington, to his family and a job.

Jennifer and her husband, Bill, did agree to let Michael live with them until he could get back on his feet. One day, when Bill was driving Michael to a job interview, he looked him in the eye and said, "You're high, aren't you? You don't need a job. You need help. I can't take you to this interview in your current condition."

Bill took Michael back home. He spent two days in withdrawal, sick and weak, until a bed opened for him at a detox center. He stayed there for five days and then moved into an inpatient treatment program where he stayed for a month. Fortunately, Michael's sister had him enrolled in an insurance program through the Affordable Care Act. Michael had the appropriate medical and mental health help that he desperately needed.

Once Michael graduated from his treatment program, he moved back in with Jennifer and Bill. He quickly found a 12-step program near his home and attended faithfully. Through this program, Michael was able to connect with Adam M. (profiled in Chapter 1) and learned about the King County job readiness training program. Although Michael wasn't officially enrolled in the program, he faithfully attended all four days of the workshop.

On the first day of class, Michael was one of those "I just need a job" people. As we talked about the work he had done in the past and the skills he enjoyed using, Michael kept coming back to the time he had help his friend detail automobiles. He liked using his hands, performing detailed work and seeing an immediate result of his efforts. By the end of the workshop, he had decided that detailing cars was something he enjoyed, an occupation that was easily available to him and one he could eventually turn into his own business.

The class invigorated Michael and he started feeling hopeful about his future. Over the weekend, he polished his resume and identified a few car dealerships close to home. He practiced his commercial (branding statement) and how he would address questions about his background. He did want his employer to know that he was in recovery and had been clean and sober for over six months.

On Monday, Michael put on a nice pair of pants, a collared shirt and left his signature baseball cap at home. He felt professional and ready to work. With resume in hand, he walked to a car dealership two blocks from his house and asked to speak to the manager. The manager was impressed by his appearance and honesty. By the end of the day, Michael had a new job detailing cars.

I had lunch with Michael about a month after he started working. He was enjoying his new job and trying to learn everything he could about the detailing business. His goal is to save enough money to buy a vehicle and the equipment he needs to start a mobile detailing operation. Then he hopes to get back to his music and do a little traveling. He is clean, sober and doing work he enjoys. He is excited about his future.

Comments from Michael:

One of my biggest problems as an addict was asking for help. I kept thinking that all I needed was a job, but I needed much more than that. Getting into recovery was the critical first step in turning my life around. I was fortunate to have family who still cared about me and didn't give up on me. They were able to get me the help I needed, and I don't want to let them down.

It was the job readiness workshop that helped me identify a job that I would enjoy. I was your ultimate job hopper working as a handy man, landscaper and a lot of other short-time jobs. The detailing work I did for my friend was something I excelled at and enjoyed. Once I landed on this career goal and saw a future for myself, I felt hopeful and motivated. With the tips and tricks I learned in the job readiness class, I was confident and ready to find a job.

Advice from Terry:

Don't let the job application screen you out.

Michael took a proactive approach to finding a detailing job. Instead of going online and filling out job applications, he focused his resume for detailing jobs, identified the auto dealerships close to home and then walked in and presented himself to the hiring manager, before he filled out a job application.

Most job applications are designed to screen out job applicants, especially those with a criminal record and should be avoided, if possible, until after an interview. Michael is proof that walking in with a resume and handing it to the hiring manager, in person, is a highly effective job search strategy. It gives the hiring manager a chance to meet you face-to-face, and you have an opportunity to make a good first impression before you bring up your background.

If walking in isn't possible, try to identify the hiring manager or recruiter of the company you have targeted. Address your cover letter to that person and include your resume. First send your cover letter and resume by email as requested in the job posting. Then send it by fax or U.S. mail marked "second submission" to the company contact you have identified. You want to make sure a physical copy of your cover letter and resume get into the hands of a real live person. Although many companies discourage phone calls, if they don't explicitly say it, a follow-up phone call won't hurt.

If filling out a job application is your only alternative, here are some tips to avoid being screened out of consideration:

Appearance

If you are submitting a paper application (very rare these days but preferable to the electronic variety) make sure there are no coffee stains, torn corners and crossed-out words. First impressions count on paper as well as in person. It is best to ask for two applications. Use one for practice, then copy the information to a clean document, keeping the original for your file. If you walk into a company to fill out a job application, make sure you bring a black or blue pen, a master application with employment dates, addresses and phone numbers, correction fluid to cover errors and a dictionary. Avoid asking the Human Resources person for a pen when you walk in to fill out a job application. This will make you look unprepared and unprofessional. Dress the part when you are applying for a job. The minute you walk into a company, people are forming their impressions of you.

If you are filling out a job application online, remember to print out a copy for your file. Each job application will be a little different. You want to keep a record of the information you gave to each employer. Don't rely exclusively on spell-check. Proof-read your application carefully before submitting.

Personal information

It is illegal for employers to ask your age, marital status and ethnicity on a job application. However, they often like to gather that data to be eligible for tax credits. Generally, this information is collected separately from your job application and considered optional. Fill it out only if you think it is to your advantage to do so; otherwise, avoid it.

The Social Security number is often requested on a job application, but employers don't need this information unless you are a job finalist and a background check is required. Because identify theft is common today, most employers make this information optional until they need it. In the blank space that asks for your Social Security number, write in "Available at interview." This lets the reader know that you haven't skipped the request; you are just waiting until the interview to provide this information.

Because of the cost, most employers don't do background checks until after they have interviewed a candidate and are pretty sure they want to make an offer. This allows you to warn a potential employer about your past in advance, so there are no surprises when the background check comes back with a report of your past conviction(s). If you are filling out an electronic application, skip the social security number request unless it is a required field and you don't have an option.

Have you ever been convicted of a crime?

This is the question all ex-offenders dread. It is definitely meant to screen out law-breakers or at least raise a red flag. Like Michael demonstrated, meeting the employer and getting him or her to like you prior to filling out a job application can render this question moot.

Some job applications will add a time limit for convictions of seven or 10 years. Others will distinguish between a felony and a misdemeanor. Read the question carefully. Then you have two options. (Lying is not one of them.) You can leave the question blank and explain your record in the interview, or you can respond with one of the following phrases:

- Yes, will explain at interview
- Yes, have met all legal obligations
- Yes, prior to ... (add a date if it has been more than 10 years)

Do not go into a lengthy explanation. It won't help and can only hurt your cause.

It may be worth your while to pay for a background check on yourself so you know what the employer will find. Check with your state patrol office or The National H.I.R.E Network to locate a reliable version of your rap sheet.

Reasons for leaving your last job.

Keep this answer brief and general. Avoid using terms like "more money," or "personality conflict." Acceptable answers are "New opportunity," "Relocated," "Career Change," or "Retraining." If you were doing seasonal or contract work, were laid off or the company closed, it is OK to say so. If the application asks you explicitly if you were ever fired from a job, if it applies, respond with "yes, not a good fit." Keep it simple, but be prepared to explain if the question comes up again in an interview.

The salary question

Depending on how you answer this question, it may automatically eliminate your chance for an interview or get you a job offer substantially below market rate. Therefore, it is best to avoid putting numbers on the job application. If the application asks for the salary desired, your response should be "open" or "negotiable." However, job applications often asks a beginning and ending salary for at each job. If you had jobs that paid wages substantially higher than the employer is offering, the employer will probably remove your application from consideration—assuming you cost too much. If you were making minimum wage (or twenty-five cents an hour working in a prison kitchen) you don't want to state that either or there is a chance you will be "low-balled" when negotiating compensation. The safest response is to put "market rate" in the salary section for each job. If you are filling out an electronic application, and are forced to commit to a salary range, do your research first to find out what the job market is currently paying the type of job you are applying for.

References

Make sure you have three strong advocates to list in the reference section of the job application. These can be former bosses, teachers, clergy, co-workers, vendors, staff you supervised and customers. If you have been volunteering, ask the volunteer coordinator for a reference. Always get permission from your references first and inform them if they are about to get called. It is OK to coach your references by giving them the job description, a copy of your resume and filling them in on the skills and attributes the employer is looking for.

Ask good questions.

When Michael walked into the car dealership, he wasn't expecting to meet the hiring manager, but he was prepared if he had the opportunity to do so. He had already researched the dealership on the Internet, rehearsed his commercial and practiced his answers to difficult questions. And as he had learned in his job readiness training class, he had a list of questions to ask the employer.

Asking questions in a job interview is almost as important as having good responses to the questions being asked. By preparing a list of questions to ask the interviewer, you demonstrate your interest in the company and curious nature. Avoid asking questions about salary, benefits and sick leave policies. Do ask questions related to the company and the job. Here are suggested question you can choose from. Pick three or four from each category, others may come up naturally during the interview.

About the company:
- What kinds of challenges is your company facing in the next year?
- What does it take to be successful in your company?
- How would you describe the culture of your company?
- What kind of training does your company provide?
- How does your company reward exceptional performance?

About the job:
- What would a typical day on the job look like?
- Who would I report to?
- Why is this position open?
- Is there an internal candidate?
- How would your describe the team culture?

About the process:
- How do you feel my qualifications fit with this position?
- What are the next steps in the hiring process?
- When can I expect to hear from you?
- May I contact you if I have additional questions?

Although many of your questions may get answered during the interview, don't come up short when the employers says, "Do you have any questions you'd like to ask us?" If you have enough questions prepared in advance, it will take only one or two to show you are an intelligent and well prepared job candidate, and a strong job contender.

Consider self-employment and freelance work

There are subtle differences between owning your own business and freelancing, based on how you structure your work physically and for tax purposes. A business owner may own a storefront. Freelancers often work out of their home. I am using the terms interchangeable here to mean being your own boss and working for many clients or customers.

Self-employment has its advantages. For one, rarely do your customers require a background check. It also fills the gap from prison to employment on your resume. Freelancing allows you the freedom to work a variety of jobs on your terms. The downside is that it is hard to get a business off the ground if you don't have capital or marketing savvy.

Michael's end goal is to start is own detailing business. For now, he is taking it slow, learning the ropes and building his capital. Keeping his day job is a prudent approach, and one I highly recommend, as he methodically builds his business on the side.

Fortunately, many businesses don't require a lot of overhead and there are free resources to assist you with marketing. Start with the Small Business Administration (SBA) at www.sba.gov. There are offices in every state. The SBA website has all the information and forms you will need to start your own business. But don't stop there. Be sure to make an appointment with a SCORE counselor. These counselors are retired business executives who volunteer for the SBA and serve as mentors to new entrepreneurs. Depending on where you live, you may work with a SCORE counselor in person, usually at a library, on the phone or, most typically, online. You can find out more about SCORE and how to get invaluable (and free) business advice at the SBA website.

The Take-aways:

- ✓ Take time to brainstorm career ideas with others. Think about what you like to do and how that can transfer to a job you will love.
- ✓ Identify employers close to home and just walk in. Demonstrate professionalism and confidence.
- ✓ Start with a resume and cover letter. Avoid job applications if possible.
- ✓ Consider working for yourself to fill an employment gap or as a future goal.

Chapter 12
POSTSCRIPTS

Most students who complete my class go out into the world and I rarely hear from them again. I often wonder what happened to the former bank robbing grandmother, homeless army vet and smooth talking drug dealer who populated my classes for four days. Did they find employment? Are they back in prison? Have their lives changed at all for the better? Many of their stories stay with me long after their names and faces disappear from memory. Although I don't know the final chapters of their stories, there are a few anecdotes that stick in my mind and are worth sharing. They reinforce many of the themes described previously in this book.

Henry: Just walk in and ask.

Henry was a shy, Hispanic man in his mid-twenties. After my class, he planned to train as an asbestos removal worker. He had some experience working on cars, but his work history was pretty sketchy. Quiet and unexpressive, it was difficult for me to know if any of the information being imparted in class was getting through to him. During the first three days of class, he only spoke when called upon.

Then, on the last day of class, Henry walked into the classroom and announced, "Miss Terry, I did what you said and walked into an auto body shop near my house after class yesterday. I told them I needed a part-time job in the evenings and weekends while I was going to school. I said I was the best person for the job because I was dependable, a good problem solver and mechanical. I also told them I could be bonded through the Federal Bonding Program, and they would get tax credits for hiring me because of my record. They hired me on the spot."

It was like having a new student in class. This unobtrusive man suddenly glowed with confidence. By the last day of class he had become an employment expert and was knowingly advising his classmates on how to conduct an effective job search.

Albert: Identifying marketable skills through your stories.

The large, bald white man in the corner of the room was a canvas of tattoos and had a sumo wrestler presence. This was one of the very first classes in which I was working with ex-offenders, and I had to admit, Albert was definitely intimidating. As was my protocol, I went around the room and asked each student to state his name and the type of job he was looking for. When I got to Albert, he looked at me as if I had asked if he had been to the moon. "I have been locked up for ten years for selling drugs. I have no skills that an employer is going to want."

Pretending to be unfazed by his belligerence, I asked Albert if he had a job while in prison. As it turned out, he worked in the prison kitchen for most of his incarceration. With some probing, Albert revealed he had cooked meals for as many as 300 inmates. He had modified recipes using basic math, substituted ingredients when stock was short and was versed in sanitizing equipment and the safe food handling guidelines required by the State. "Maybe I do have something to offer," Albert said with a hint of a smile. From that point on, I had him. Albert was animated, engaged and hopeful that a career as a cook would be in his future.

Margie: Rewards of networking.

Margie, a legal assistant, was not an ex-offender, but one of my private clients. Her story is worth noting here as it is one we all can learn from. She was the shy type, the kind of person you had to pry information out of. When it came to the topic of networking, I practically had to restrain her from running out of my office. After a little bit of probing Margie finally told me, "I am just uncomfortable talking about myself. I never know what to say, and I hate to sound like I am bragging."

After some persuasion on my part, Margie agreed to let me help her create a "commercial" or script she could use when talking to strangers about her job search. Her commercial included the type of work she was looking for and why she was good at it. It was about 30 seconds long and simple to remember without sounding rehearsed. I asked Margie to share her commercial with her friends and relatives first. When she felt comfortable with it, she should try it out with others in casual conversation, her hairdresser, perhaps, or the grocery store clerk she sees on a regular basis.

Several weeks later I got a phone call from Margie. She had been at an air show over the weekend. While waiting in line at the concession stand to buy a hot dog, she mustered up the courage to try her commercial on the man behind the counter taking orders. She told him she was new to the area and looking for a job as a legal assistant. She could type 60 words per minute, answer multiple phone lines and had great organizational and customer service skills. The man in the white paper hat and apron looked at her with a smile. He said, "I am volunteering today, but in my day job I am a lawyer, and I happen to be looking for an office assistant. Would you like to come to my office next week for an interview?"

Margie interviewed and accepted a job offer. When she called me she said, "I want you to share my story with your students. Networking works."

Ahmed: Thank you goes a long way.

Ahmed was unusually attentive when I was discussing the value of writing a thank you note to an employer after an interview. Most people don't think to do this, which is one reason why writing a thank you note is so powerful. It sets you apart from the herd of job candidates. At one point in the discussion, Ahmed raised his hand and asked, "When should you write the thank you note? I interviewed for a warehouse job at Pepsi Cola two weeks ago. Is it too late to write one?"

I told Ahmed, it is best to write a thank you note within 24-hours of the meeting and that the job he had interviewed for was probably filled. But I also told him it was never too late to thank someone for his or her time and express interest in working for the company.

After class, Ahmed showed me a thank you note he had handwritten in pencil on lined notebook paper. He asked me to proof-read it to correct spelling and grammar. I assumed he was going to go home, type the letter and mail it to the hiring manager with whom he had interviewed at the Pepsi warehouse.

The next day in class, we were discussing the hidden job market when Ahmed's mother appeared at the door. She motioned for Ahmed to come outside. As it turned out, Ahmed had personally delivered his handwritten thank you note on his way home from class the previous day. Early the next morning, the Pepsi hiring manager called Ahmed's home to offer him a job. Was it a coincidence that Ahmed received this call a day after delivering his thank note, or did his note have an impact on the hiring manager's decision making? You decide.

Angela: Nice offer; poor fit.

Confident and articulate, Angela was a 30-something bookkeeper who appeared well-put-together professionally. In fact, she was a recovering alcoholic who had "done time" for bank robbery. When I met Angela, she was living in a half-way house and making a full-time job out of looking for a job. She spent a good portion of her day online applying for call-center and office support jobs. Because she had mastered the art of resume writing, she had an unusually high response rate to her online job applications. After she applied to one call-center job through a staffing agency, the recruiter called while Angela was in my class. She said the call center hiring manager of a large, national bank wanted to interview her. Angela told the recruiter she couldn't talk at the moment and would call her back.

"This is crazy," Angela said during our lunch break. "With my background, I can't work for a bank."

"Be up front with the recruiter, and let her know you have a record," I suggested. "That way you won't appear to be hiding anything, and you won't be wasting her time or yours."

Angela called the recruiter back immediately. I overheard her tell the woman that she wouldn't be able to pass a background check due to a past conviction. Apparently, the recruiter appreciated Angela's honesty and told her to go to the interview regardless. Angela and I were nonplused, but she decided to follow through.

In the end, Angela aced the interview and received a job offer from the bank. It was her parole officer that intervened and reminded her it was a violation of her parole to take this kind of job. Always the optimist, Angela saw this job offer as a victory, proof that she was employable. Now she just had to find the right fit.

Cliff: Just show up.

The construction industry is a very forgiving industry when it comes to employing individuals with criminal backgrounds. But in today's marketplace, job seekers still have to overcome the hurdle of getting the interview. Prior to his incarceration, Cliff never had trouble getting a construction job. But after being incarcerated for 12 years, looking for a job was a new ball game. Cliff had applied online for dozens of construction jobs without a nibble. He was extremely frustrated and starting to feel desperate.

Finally one morning Cliff got up early, put on his jeans, a clean work shirt and some hard toed boots. He headed to a commercial construction site not too far from home where a large multi-use complex was being built. He found the site foreman and told him he was prepared to work. As it happened, a couple of crew members failed to show up that morning. The foreman agreed to try Cliff out and by the end of the day, Cliff had a new job.

Gilbert: Taking the first step.

About a year after taking my class, Gilbert contacted me to let me know how he was doing. He had gone through a recovery program and was back on track, taking a few classes to update his computer skills.

Six months later, I contacted Gilbert to find out if he was employed. He was still taking classes and working on his resume. It was becoming clear that Gilbert was scared to look for work. Taking classes and continually refining his resume were avoidance tactics.

After Gilbert sent one of several resume drafts, I finally wrote back with the message, "Just send it." Sometimes *good enough* is better than *just perfect*. Gilbert took the leap. He applied for a job online and attached his resume, which quickly resulted in his first job interview after many years.

Although he didn't get an offer, he did gain much needed confidence. He continues to "tweak" his resume, but he is also more proactive about getting it into the hands of employers.

Audrey: Closing the job gaps.

A big problem for ex-offenders is the gap an incarceration creates on a resume. Many individuals work while in prison and there are techniques for presenting prison jobs on a resume without making it obvious the candidate was an inmate. But some inmates don't work while incarcerated or struggle to find employment once they are released, creating a gap in their work history of several years.

Audrey was one of these individuals who had a sketchy work history. She had odd jobs in customer service and telemarketing, but they never lasted very long nor had she worked in the last four years. She also had a couple of brief jobs in prison, but mainly she took classes and worked on her personal development.

During break, I overheard Audrey talking on her cell phone. She was asking the caller questions about the length, color and texture of her hair. When the call ended, I casually asked Audrey if she cut hair? "Oh, I've been styling hair for years. Mostly friends and relatives. I even did the gals in prison. Here is my business card."

Audrey hadn't recognized that her hobby or freelance work as a hair stylist was legitimate work and the perfect job to put on her resume to fill an employment gap. Whether she got paid for her work or did if for free, she was using a number of marketable skills that would be valuable to an employer.

If the hole between your last job is expanding, create your own work. Wash windows, cut lawns, walk dogs or clean houses. Form your own "free-lance" business to fill the gap on your resume, showcase your skills and entrepreneurial spirit and prove to employers that you are not the kind of person to just sit around.

Randy: Many rewards of volunteering.

Randy spent seven years in prison playing pinochle. He was bright, strategic, had a great memory and terrific math skills, which attributed to his card playing acumen. We struggled for a way to present these attributes on his resume, but there was really no honest way to spin "card shark" into a legitimate career.

It wasn't until the last day of class that Randy let slip that he was volunteering for a nonprofit that recycled computers. He was in charge of taking computers apart and inventorying parts. He often worked alone and was accountable for several thousands of dollars of recyclable material. Randy had finally recognized that he did have viable work experience and skills that could be translated to a resume in an acceptable way. It didn't matter that he wasn't receiving a paycheck. His volunteer work provided tangible proof that he was productive and trustworthy.

Pete: Mind your spin

During one workshop, I asked a student, Pete, if he would volunteer to talk about his conviction. "Sure," he said. "I got busted for drug trafficking." My mind immediately conjured up an image of Pete driving across the Mexican border in the dark of night with bricks of heroin stashed in the spare tire of his Honda. To me, someone with little experience with the law, the words *drug trafficking* sounded like a very serious offense. After hearing more details and with a little bit of coaching, I again asked Pete to tell me about his conviction. He responded, "I made a very bad choice and got caught selling marijuana to some friends." This time the image in my mind is of me, sharing a joint with my friends back in college and almost getting caught by the cops. Now Pete doesn't seem like such a criminal after all, and I can empathize with his unfortunate incarceration. How you "spin" your stories in an interview can have a big impact on the listener's decision to hire you.

Laura: Do your research.

Laura had an interview scheduled for a wait staff position with a fine-dining establishment. Prior to the interview, she went on the restaurant website and absorbed as much as she could about the company. She learned that the name of the restaurant came from Greek mythology, she studied the business mission and memorized the menu. Next, she made a visit the restaurant. Although she couldn't afford to eat there, she casually observed the customers coming in and out and caught a glimpse here and there of the wait staff.

On the day of the interview, Laura dressed in black pants and white shirt. She wore a skinny black tie, like she had seen the restaurant employees wearing. When she walked into the interview, it was as if she already worked there. She was hired on the spot, bypassing a background check. Even the hiring manager was surprised to learn how the company he had been working at for several years got its name.

RESOURCES

Government Sponsored Programs

American Job Center

http://jobcenter.usa.gov/about-us

This site provides a single access point to key federal programs and critical local resources to help people find a job, identify training programs, and gain skills in growing industries. It connects individuals to online resources and hundreds of local training programs and job resources funded through federal grants.

Bureau of Labor Statistics

www.bls.gov

The Bureau of Labor Statistics of the U.S. Department of Labor is the principal Federal agency responsible for measuring labor market activity, working conditions, and price changes in the economy. Since 1884, it has collected, analyzed, and disseminated essential economic information to support public and private decision-making. It is a good resource to determine the employment outlook for various careers as well as obtain detailed information about specific occupations and wages.

Career One Stop

www.careeronestop.org

This website is sponsored by the U.S. Department of Labor. It will help you identify the state employment agency closest to your zip code. These one-stop employment centers help job seekers with career exploration, job finding, worker retraining programs, unemployment compensation and much more. It can also refer you to resources and programs designed specifically for individuals with criminal records.

Department of Licensing

If you drivers license is suspended due to unpaid traffic tickets or other circumstances, it can be an enormous barrier to finding and accepting a job. Contact the Department of Licensing in your state to inquire about how to get your license back. Most states will issue Occupational or Restricted licenses until you are fully reinstated.

Employment Security
Federal Bonding Program
www.bonds4jobs.com
In 1966, the U.S. Department of Labor established The Federal Bonding Program to provide Fidelity Bonds that guarantee honesty for "at-risk," hard-to-place job seekers and those with criminal records. The bonds cover the first six months of employment. There is no cost to the job applicant or the employer, but arrangements must be made prior to the employee's first day on the job. In most states the bonds are made available through the state agency responsible for workforce matters.

National H.I.R.E. Network
www.hirenetwork.org
Established by the Legal Action Center in 2001, the National Helping Individuals with criminal records Re-enter through Employment (H.I.R.E.) Network is both a national clearinghouse for information and an advocate for policy change. The goal of the National H.I.R.E. Network is to increase the number and quality of job opportunities available to people with criminal records by changing public policies, employment practices and public opinion. The website's Clearinghouse provides resources, information and assistance by state. It includes state-specific government and community based organizations to assist people with criminal records by providing job-related and legal services, answering questions arising from having a criminal record, or offering referrals to other useful organizations.

National Re-entry Resource Center
Council of State Government Justice Center
www.csgjusticecenter.org
The National Re-entry Resource Center is a part of the Council of State Government Justice Center. It provides education, training and technical assistance to states, tribes, territories, local governments, service providers, non-profit organizations, and corrections institutions working on prisoner reentry. The Reentry Services Directory was developed to help individuals who have been incarcerated and their families find local reentry services. The NRRC has compiled a list of organizations and service providers who can address different reentry needs, including housing, employment, and family reunification. The website has a map where you can locate services offered in your state. The link is http://csgjusticecenter.org/reentry/reentry-services-directory

SafeLink Wireless
www.safelinkwirless.com
SafeLink Wireless is a LifeLine government benefit service, a program of the Federal Communication Commission. Low income individuals apply for eligibility. It offers free cell phones, unlimited text messaging and 500 free minutes for four months and then unlimited text messaging and 350 minutes a month thereafter. It is limited to one per household.

Small Business Administration
www.sba.gov
The Small Business Administration has been helping entrepreneurs since 1953. It helps new business owners obtain loans and contracts for government services. It also provides counseling and other forms of assistance to small business. The S.C.O.R.E. counselors, retired business executives, volunteer their time to consult with small business owners. The Small Business Resource magazine is the most complete guide to starting and expanding

your business. You'll find information on counseling, training, capital, contracting, disaster assistance, business advocacy, local directories and more. Visit the SBA website to find the a regional office near you.

U.S. Department of Justice

Federal Bureau of Investigation Information Services Division
www.fbi.gov/about-us/cjis/identity-history-summary-checks
When you are fingerprinted by a law enforcement agency, this information is sent to a central repository in the state where you committed the crime. If you have committed crimes in several states your "rap sheet" will be on file with the FBI's Interstate Identification Index. It is important to know what an employer will find when they do a background check or if your crimes will make you ineligible for certain types of jobs. You may even find a few mistakes that need to be corrected. To obtain a copy of your rap sheet at the federal and state levels contact the FBI Information Services Division at the email above.

U.S. Department of Veteran Affairs

http://www.benefits.va.gov/vocrehab/
If your are a veteran, you may receive be eligible to receive vocational rehabilitation and employment services to help with job training, employment accommodations, resume development, and job seeking skills coaching. Other services may be provided to assist veterans in starting their own businesses or independent living services for those who are severely disabled and unable to work in traditional employment.

Veteran's Administration

http://www.va.gov/jobs/
Recognizing the sacrifices made by those serving in the military, the Veteran's administration has a variety of resources and programs for veterans who are unemployed, homeless and reentering the job market after incarceration.

Work Opportunity Tax Credit

www.doleta.gov

The Work Opportunity Tax Credit (WOTC) is a Federal tax credit available to employers for hiring individuals from certain target groups who have consistently faced significant barriers to employment. Employers hiring ex-offenders who have been convicted or released from prison within one year of the date of hire, and are a member of a low-income family, qualify for a tax credit off the bottom-line at the end of the business year.

Online Career Resources

Addiction Recovery Guide

www.addictionrecoveryguide.org

12-Step programs offer guiding principles to help individuals tackling problems and receive support related to their additions. Most are spiritual in nature. Alcoholics Anonymous (AA) was the first such program, but many others, such as Narcotics Anonymous (NA) and Gamblers Anonymous (GA) have used the 12-Step methodology as their foundation. Many of the people profiled in this book remain members of a 12-Step program as it keeps them connected to others and keeps them grounded. To find a 12-Step program to meet your specific needs refer to the Addiction Recovery Guide. Resources are listed by state.

Employment Information Handbook

Bureau of Prisons

www.bop/resources

Designed for ex-offenders, this employment handbook is available on the BOP website under resources for ex-offenders.

Occupational Outlook Handbook

www.bls.gov/oco

O*Net Dictionary of Occupational Titles

www.onetonline.org

If you aren't sure what kind of job you want or what is available based on your skills and abilities, the two above resources are great tools for career exploration.

The *Occupational Outlook Handbook* is a published by the United States Department of Labor's Bureau of Labor Statistics. It provides an overview of nearly 250 occupations that account for 87 percent of the nations jobs. It includes information about the nature of work, working conditions, training and education, earnings and job outlook for hundreds of different occupations in the United States. It is a good resource to understand the skills, abilities, knowledge and educational requirements of an occupation as well as wage information and future growth rates.

Also published by the U.S. Department of Labor, is the O*Net Dictionary of Occupational Titles. This online resource identifies, in depth, as many as 1,100 job titles. It includes skills assessment activities and has a special section to help veterans assess their transferable skills to non-military occupations.

Pacer's National Parent Center on Transition and Employment Vocational Rehabilitation Services

www.pacer.org

This website provides high quality assistance and support to parents, youth, and professionals on transition topics pertaining to education and employment for those with disabilities. It has an excellent resource page for finding state vocational rehabilitation programs.

http://www.parac.org/svrp.html

Community-based Programs and Resources

AARP Foundation WorkSearch

www.aarpworksearch.org

This free program sponsored by American Association of Retired Persons (AARP), offers employment and training services to workers age 55 and older who meet residential and income eligibility. Having a felony will not disqualify you. Programs may vary from state to state, but AARP claims to have the highest placement rate of all older worker job placement programs in the U.S.

Apprenticeship and Non-traditional Employment for Women (ANEW)

www.anewaop.org

In partnership with local trade unions, ANEW provides women of all ages, races, and backgrounds with quality training, support services and employment preparation, leading to viable and satisfying non-traditional career pathways which lead to living-wage jobs.

Goodwill Industries

www.goodwill.org

There are 165 independently based Goodwill outlets around the country, so you can find one in most major cities. The organization is all about second chances and offers a diverse array of pre-release services including assistance obtaining a GED, English as a Second Language (ESL) classes, employment readiness and occupational skills training, financial consulting and job placement.

National Mentoring Partnership

www.mentoring.org

The National Mentoring Partnerships has 5,000 programs in 50 states. The national organizations helps local programs with resources and tools to support mentorship programs. You can find a program near you by visiting the national website.

Oxford House

www.oxfordhouse.us

Oxford House is a group of self-run, self-supported recovery houses that offer recovering individuals a place to live and the safe environment needed to stay clean and sober. Trained outreach workers are on staff to provide support services. This website will provide a map to help you located the Oxford House in your geographic area.

Salvation Army

www.salvationarmyusa.org

For over 100 years The Salvation Army's Adult Rehabilitation Centers and Harbor Light programs have been providing spiritual, social and emotional assistance for men and women who are unable cope with their problems and take care of themselves. Centers offer residential housing, work, and group and individual therapy. Many offer employment assistance, job search training and interview clothing.

Toastmasters International

www.toastmaters.org

Toastmasters has over 15,000 chapters in a 135 countries. Its mission is to "provide a supportive and positive learning experience in which members are empowered to develop communication and leadership skills, resulting in greater self-confidence and personal growth." Many prisons have Toastmaster programs and you can find at least one in almost every community. It is a safe and friendly way to improve your communication skills and gain confidence. It is also a good place to find a professional mentor.

United Way

www.unitedway.org

When you don't know where to turn, contact the United Way chapter nearest you. United Way will connect you to partner agencies that can help you with housing, health care, substance abuse, employment, child or elder care or an other issues that may disrupting your well-being. Many local United Way agencies can be accessed by dialing 2-1-1. United Way can also connect you to volunteer opportunities that will match your interest and skills.

Job Assistance Websites

Craig's List

www.craigslist.com

Unfortunately, this popular website has become a breeding ground for job scams, multi-level marketing schemes and other illegitimate job postings. However, it does have its place in your job search tool kit if you are looking for quick, one-time, pick up work to make a fast buck. At the bottom of the employment list is a section called "Gigs." There are trade gigs, event gigs, labor gigs, even writing and talent gigs. Perhaps a movie is being filmed in your city and there is a need for a multitude of "extras," or a major event is coming to your area and the event managers are in need of a crew to help set-up and break-down the venue. These are the kinds of jobs you might find on "Gigs."

If you use this job board, be sure to read all job postings carefully. If the job sounds ambiguous or there is no employer or contact information listed, be wary and proceed cautiously.

Glassdoor

www.glassdoor.com

Glassdoor has a database of more than 8 million company reviews, CEO approval ratings, salary reports, interview reviews and questions, benefits reviews, office photos and more. What makes this different than other job sites is that the information posted on Glassdoor comes from employees of the companies profiled. If you are wondering what it is like to work for a specific company, this is a good place to get "insider" information.

Hard to Hire

www.hardtohire.com

Specifically for ex-offenders, in addition to national job postings, this website offers advice on the types of jobs available to ex-offenders, related websites and franchise information for individuals wanting to start their own business.

Indeed and Simply Hired

www.indeed.com

www.simplyhired.com

Pick one of these websites and that is probably all you need to conduct an online job search. Both are employment related search engines for job listings. They aggregate postings from thousands of sites including job boards such as Monster and CareerBuilder, staffing agencies and individual company websites. Pick the one you like the best and you don't need to use any other job boards. You find jobs close to home by entering key words and your zip code. You can also indicate how far you want to commute, 10, 15, 25 or 50 miles. Both sites also provide salary comparisons and other valuable job information such as commonly used job titles or the number of new openings in your area. This is an especially good tool if you want to relocate to another state and need to research the kinds of employers and jobs that are available

Job Hunters Bible

www.jobhuntersbible.com

This website was created by Richard Bolles, the author of *What Color is My*

Parachute?, the definitive guide for job hunters. It includes an career interest inventory and lists of books and resources to aid you in your job search.

LinkedIn

www.linkedin.com

This is a social media website mainly used by business professionals. It claims 364 million members across 200 counties and 24 languages. Users create a professional profile and link to other professionals. The site can be used to find people in companies, learn about job openings, participate in online discussions related to your field and announce professional achievements. Many LinkedIn users post recommendations they have received from professional contacts.

Security is fairly stringent and you are not obligated to accept invitations. My rule of thumb is to accept invitations from people you know, people connected to people you know, or professionals in your field. Be sure to include a professional looking photo and profile. Recruiters and hiring managers increasingly use LinkedIn to find job candidates or as a reference point before inviting you in to an interview.

Riley Guide

www.rileyguide.com

Created by a librarian, the Riley Guide provides over 1600 links to job related websites. It links you to resources related to career exploration, employers, resumes and cover letters, dealing with job loss, salary guides and much more.

Volunteer Match

www.volunteermatch.org

If you are looking for a volunteer opportunity close to home, this is the website you will want to visit. Just enter your zip code, geographic parameters and key words that match the cause you care about and Volunteer Match will provide you with agencies and events that need your services. In some cases, you may have to apply with a resume and complete a background check, but there are plenty of opportunities to simply express your interest in an email and then show up.

Recommended Reading

The following books can be purchased through your favorite online book dealer or, in most cases, found at your local library. They are available in print and ebook formats.

Playing the Job Finding Game: A rule book for ex-offenders, by Terry Pile
A step-by-step guide based on my job readiness training workshop, this workbook is filled with advice, exercises, templates, tips and success stories. It was written specifically for anyone who can't pass a background check to. It will help you to think like an employer, identify your marketable skills, develop a job finding game plan, craft effective resumes and cover letters, break into the hidden job market with appropriate job finding strategies and respond to the killer interview questions. This book is guaranteed to get you into shape for playing the job finding game—and come out a winner.

What Color is Your Parachute? By Richard Nelson Bolles
A classic job finding resource, this book is on every career counselors bookshelf and serves as the job hunter's bible. (Also the name of Bolles website www.jobhuntersbible.com.) Much of the book is devoted to helping job hunters and career changers find the work they love, but it also includes practical advice about finding hiring managers, interviewing techniques and salary negotiations. This book is updated almost annually, so try to find the most current addition you can. Although the core information doesn't change, websites and other resources do.

Best Resumes & Letters for Ex-offenders, by Wendy S. Enelow and Ronald Krannich
Part of the "Overcoming Barriers to Employment Series" published by Im-

pact Publications, this book is filled with resume and cover letter examples
that address the specific concerns of ex-offenders. It will help you develop a
well-crafted resume and cover letter that communicates your qualifications
in a way that employers will want to meet you. It includes key principles of
resume writing, mistakes to avoid, resume worksheets and a list of action
verbs and personal descriptors to help you describe your skills and abilities.

The Ex-offenders' Job Interview Guide, by Caryl and Ron Krannich, Ph.Ds
A critical component to landing a job is doing well in an interview. This
guide is filled with interview advice for individuals who are re-entering the
job market. It includes a list of over 100 frequently asked interview questions and offers advice on answering the difficult ones such as "Have you
ever been convicted of a felony?" "How do I know I can trust you?' "Tell me
about yourself." It also covers common job search and interview mistakes
ex-offenders make, nonverbal interview behaviors and tips for negotiating
salary and benefits.

ABOUT THE AUTHOR

Terry Pile is a creative and versatile career counselor and coach specializing in helping people find and succeed in the work they love. She has been working with individuals and businesses throughout the U.S. for over a decade. She began working with the ex-offender population through the King County Jobs Initiative in 2006.

Terry has a Master's degree in education from Indiana University and a certificate in career development facilitation from the University of Washington. She is certified by the Center for Credentialing and Education as a Global Career Development Facilitator (GCDF). Career counseling is Terry's third career. She taught in the public schools and was a marketing executive at Ogilvy & Mather Worldwide. Now she teaches individuals to market themselves for successful employment.

In addition, to consulting and training, Terry writes feature articles on career issues in the print and electronic media. She has published five electronic books on career topics through Get to the Point Books, www.gettothepoint-books.com. She is the co-author of *Changing Careers after 40: Real Stories, New Callings, Playing the Job Finding Game: A rule book for ex-offenders,* and *Essential Advice for Finding Better Jobs and Changing Careers.*

To contact Terry, visit her Web site at www.careeradvisorsonline.com.